A Fly in Milk

(UNA MOSCA EN LA LECHE)

From Eagle Pass, Texas to Washington D.C.

Victor Vasquez

Published by SuburbanBuzz.com LLC

ISBN: 978-1-959446-38-5

DEDICATION

This book is dedicated with profound gratitude and admiration to those that served as the stability in my life: my father, whose unwavering presence and boundless wisdom shaped my journey; my cherished aunts and uncles, whose nurturing embrace and encouragement guided my every step.

To them, I owe immeasurable thanks for their unwavering support, guidance, and love during the major milestones of my life.

In addition, beyond the circle of my family, I extend this dedication to the broader community whose influence was instrumental in shaping my path. To the dedicated teachers in middle school and high school, whose belief in my potential allowed a flame of ambition to burn within me, and to the college professors who recognized my capabilities and guided me toward the realization of my aspirations.

May this book stand as a testament to the profound impact of their collective support of family and community and their belief in me, shaping me into the person I am today.

CONTENTS

ACKNOWLEDGMENTS i

CHAPTER 1 No, Mijo, You Are Perfect 1

CHAPTER 2 Worlds Apart 7

CHAPTER 3 Memories of Matriarchs 19

CHAPTER 4 Mis Tios 33

CHAPTER 5 Mi Padre 49

CHAPTER 6 Campfire Stories 55

CHAPTER 7 Aztlán and The Seven Caves 69

CHAPTER 8 Leemel 79

CHAPTER 9 The Mix of Old and New Worlds 91

CHAPTER 10 An Impressionable Young Mind 109

CHAPTER 11 An Education 123

CHAPTER 12 Middle School 139

CHAPTER 13 High School 153

CHAPTER 14 Adulting 163

CHAPTER 15 Uncle Sam 171

CHAPTER 16 Dreams Pursued 203

CHAPTER 17 Higher Learning 213

CHAPTER 18 The Shortcut Becomes the Goal 221

CHAPTER 19 A New Race 233

CHAPTER 20 Breaking the Cycle 243

CHAPTER 21 Madre and a Full Circle 253

CONCLUSION 259

ABOUT THE AUTHOR 269

ACKNOWLEDGMENTS

This book could not have been completed without my wife, collaborator, and partner, Alma Cristina. I'm grateful for her unwavering support, and I'm deeply indebted that she stood by me through every step of this journey, embracing even the wildest of my ideas. There have been countless instances where my imagination led me from one project to another, often venturing into the realm of the seemingly absurd.

When I shared my aspiration to transform my scattered writings and random poems into a cohesive book, Alma Cristina didn't hesitate. She greeted the idea with her characteristic warm smile, silently acknowledging the audacity of my endeavor yet pledging her unwavering support. Thus began this odyssey of compiling my writings from various periods of my life, weaving together my thoughts and experiences into a narrative that imparts the wisdom gleaned from both my elders and life itself.

Thank you, mi amor, for being the foundation of this achievement.

Thanks, as well, to mi familia and the people who saw the possibility in a young boy's eyes. I am deeply grateful for the guidance that has helped me become a man who values others, cares for people, and believes in love.

CHAPTER 1
No, Mijo, You Are Perfect

Preservation of one's own culture does not require contempt of disrespect for other culture.
~ Cesar Chavez

On one scorching afternoon, amidst the sweltering heat and lush fields of the Yakima Valley in Washington State, I could see my family off in the distance. They were laughing and joking as we worked diligently, tending a thirty-acre field. Off in the distance, I could hear the rhythmic hum of sprinklers. The memory of that day is etched in my mind, vivid as yesterday.

Lost in my daydreams, I lagged the group. My gaze fixed on a young boy cycling along a dusty road adjacent to our field. A white towel fluttered from the bike's back, signifying his destination: the local swimming pool.

A pang of curiosity surged within me, prompting a realization—why did he have the freedom to enjoy the pool while I did not? At that moment, on that summer day, I vowed not to confine my life to the fields but to strive for a better, more liberating existence. I had no idea what I would do other than I wanted to be able to have the choice to go to the swimming pool whenever I got the urge.

I hail from the rural landscapes of small communities, with deep-rooted ties to Eagle Pass, Texas, a border town along the United States–Mexico border—where much of my family originates. The essence of my upbringing in small, rural agricultural communities has profoundly influenced my approach to life. Amidst the juxtaposition of cultures and struggles, I cultivated the qualities of reflection, resourcefulness, and adaptability. My family imparted the virtues of hard work, hope, and love, while my community and mentors emphasized living an ethical, integrity-driven life with honesty as its own reward.

My life's trajectory compelled me to traverse diverse socioeconomic boundaries—from living in labor camps as a farmworker until I was twenty-two to living in a boxcar while working for the railroad on a bridge crew, to labor camps in Alaska while working on the pipeline, and a fine home in Alexandria, Virginia, merely a mile from Mount Vernon. My career trajectory evolved through labor in agriculture, food service, construction, and power plants, eventually propelling me into executive and leadership roles within both the private and public sectors.

In each step of my journey, the ethos of giving back, never forgetting my roots, and honoring those who guided me has been a compass. Public service has been the lodestar of my professional career, spanning local, state, and federal domains. This commitment to service emanates from my family, instilled in me by my father—a decorated World War II veteran and former farmworker, epitomizing unconditional service.

I am drawn to causes that empower the disenfranchised, advocating for access and opportunities. As I reflect on my childhood my curiosity was aroused, questioning—why some endure arduous lives while others revel in simple joys. Despite acquiring a home with a swimming pool, symbolizing personal achievement, the lingering question persists. It's this inquiry and the undying desire to aid those in need that fuel my relentless pursuit of answers. I've chosen to express my thoughts in writing, hopeful that somewhere out there, someone holds the key to achieving the equity humanity ardently aspires to attain.

This is a tale of childhood hardships and experiences I survived by God's grace. It's a vibrant record of the legends and lore (and prophecies and predictions) of my ancestors that I learned around the campfires of my youth. It's an examination of what it means to "belong." It's also an immigration story and the result of what can be accomplished when individuals are willing to invest their valuable time in nurturing and inspiring others to dream. Some of my earliest memories are set in the fields and orchards where my family, migrant workers, toiled under the sun and braved the cold seasons, spanning both Mexico and the U.S. I often reflect on my journey through the lens of agriculture, for it was my community that planted the seed of my potential. They nurtured it, ensuring it received the care and attention it needed, watched it grow, and celebrated the harvest of my dreams. Guiding a child's spirit requires people of exceptional conviction and vision, and I was fortunate to have such special individuals in my life. Success did not come from the struggle that pitted me against the new world. I believe success came from the vision of my ancestors, who chose to leave their ancient lands and seek a better life. I followed in their footsteps. My story is one of a family that chose to abandon the oppression of war and poverty. My people sought a place to live where their children could grow up to live full lives without having to think of going off to some unknown land and fighting battles for and against global governments.

So many gave me love, affection, and positive reinforcement. My passion for equity, social justice, and the environment around me is a result of the example of an entire community that committed to these ideals. They took me, a rough stone, and polished me into a finished gem.

My admiration goes out to my family, who recognized that investing time and special attention was required to put me on a positive path and survive the challenges they knew I would face—the same challenges they had lived through. They taught me to enjoy every day no matter how poor we were, and that poverty was the result of forces created outside of our control. I learned from them that racism was often driven by fear of the loss of control, fear of unfamiliar languages, fear of foods, songs, and unknown religious practices.

A lack of knowledge or ignorance created those fears and resulted in hatred directed toward people they knew nothing about. The possibilities that every mainstream person dreams of are no different than those of young Latino children in this country. We are only waiting for the opportunity to walk through the multiple doors of opportunity that provide the luxury of choice. With the ability to choose comes an increased chance of success.

Thus, positive influences pointed me toward the future. My ancestors, my parents, aunts, uncles, and the people in the communities that I have lived in made my success possible. What will my mother and father's reward be for raising ten children? Where are the award ceremonies for the success of parenthood? Surely, they have earned treasures in the hereafter. After all, their offspring added something to the world in their special ways. It amazes me that ordinary, uncelebrated people manage to leave legacies of wisdom that strengthen humanity.

The man facing me in the mirror every morning has gained a balanced look at life, a man who understands the consequences of providing rewards rather than punishment for wrongdoing, and a man who has learned from the past. It becomes clearer, as age sneaks up on me like a cold north wind in the early fall, that without love and positive reinforcement, I would not have created a positive self-image.

My family immediately rejected any suggestion that I should lose weight when we sat around the dining table talking about dieting after a healthy dinner of enchiladas, rice, and beans.

"No, mijo, you are perfect," they insisted, even though I was twenty-five pounds overweight. That daily dose of positive reinforcement, delivered in a large cup of love, provided me the ability to resist the daily bombardment of systemic obstructions, temptations, and diversions, all of which would have made it more difficult for me to pursue my ever-changing dreams. The tool, the weapon available to me, was the trust and faith that others placed in my hands.

The man who looks at me every day in that mirror is proud of the small achievements, the little victories, like being one of the first in the family to graduate from high school. Getting that high school diploma provided me with options. College? Technical school? Graduate school? Military service? Without my high school diploma, none of these options would have been within reach.

Small victories have served as the springboard to bigger and greater challenges, one small step at a time, never looking behind me but forever looking forward. I measure success by inches, feet, or yards and make conscious decisions to tackle the miles one step at a time. I made my way through college one week at a time until the years went by, and graduation day finally faced me…and a broader future.

I take immense pride in my educational journey, commencing at the Blue Mountain Community College and the University of Oregon and culminating at Harvard University's Kennedy School of Government. Over the span of thirty years, I have honed my skills and garnered experience in public service, occupying senior executive roles. Yet, beneath these accomplishments lies a humble beginning and a fervent drive to serve and uplift marginalized individuals and communities. Now I leave you to the following chapters in which I chronicle my unusual tale with ancestral research into my early Aztec lineage, narratives and oral tradition, historical perspective, some heartfelt poetry, and most of all, a burning desire that my experiences uplift every reader.

CHAPTER 2
Worlds Apart

I've been put on the planet to serve humanity. I have to remind myself to live simply and not to overindulge, which is a constant battle in a material world.
~ Sandra Cisneros

This memoir documents a journey from one social and economic world to another. It feels as if I've traveled many worlds and have managed to compile it here on these pages, like a portal into experiences that most will never encounter. My hope is that readers live vicariously through my words, adventures, and life lessons. I am hopeful that a lot of wisdom, takeaways, twists, and turns appear in this book, courtesy of my ancestors and those I encountered on a wildly meandering path.

My journey was possible because of my family. They began their journey in Zacatecas, Mexico as a poor group of peasants willing to travel to a foreign country with a different language and culture. They worked for the right to live a life that would provide shelter and food for us all.

I traveled from a home of adobe walls and dirt floors in Mexico to harvesting fields in the West and Pacific Northwest, to Alaska and pipeline labor unions, and to the cobblestone streets of Cambridge, Massachusetts. I eventually reached Washington, D.C., to work on national programs that would impact migrant farm workers all over the country.

Yes, miraculously, I—a young child who couldn't speak

English when I started school—became a farmworker, soldier, major utility employee in a nuclear plant, a Harvard graduate, and eventually worked with the Department of Defense and the United States Department of Agriculture. Who knew I would end up on the East Coast working for two Presidents as a public servant?

There were some naysayers, one in particular. A high school counselor never believed I could reach my dreams, and it became my mission to prove him wrong. My last meeting with Mr. Wilson is still vivid in my mind. As I sat in the waiting area for students just outside the principal's office, a place typically reserved for kids waiting to get in trouble, all I could think about was to bolt out of the office and avoid the meeting. At the point when I felt that I had already been there a lifetime and was ready to give in to the thought that they were not going to let me graduate, I heard my name echo from a room down the hall. As I walked into the counselor's office, I could see that Mr. Wilson had an open manila folder in his hands staring at the contents as he told me to sit down.

The only thing crossing my mind was getting out of there without getting in trouble. Finally, Mr. Wilson looked up at me and calmly asked, "What are your plans after graduation?" My immediate response was, "I want to go to college and become an art teacher." Without any expression, he looked me in the eye and then stared at the folder and said, "Based on what I see here, you might want to think about going to technical school and becoming a mechanic." Without thinking, my immediate response was to tell him what he could do with himself using the F word, something you would only hear at an all-night bar in Alaska or on the street in the barrio. In my mind, it was a foregone conclusion that after my outburst, they would not let me graduate for sure. Fortune, however, was on my side, and for some reason, I escaped what could have been tragic.

I ultimately fulfilled my dreams through academic achievement and dedicated service to our country, both in the military and the public sector. After graduating with honors from the University of Oregon as a Phi Beta Kappa member, I made a six-hour drive back to my high school to inform that counselor of my accomplishment. Years later, after completing my master's degree at Harvard, I flew from Boston to Portland and drove another four hours to repeat the ritual—walking into the teachers' lounge to remind him just how wrong he had been. Today, I also thank him for his doubt and discouragement. It became the fuel that propelled me forward.

My goal has always been to search out multiple paths with several directions from which to choose. It was my belief that I had to consider every path placed before with only one condition, which was that any path I chose had to move ahead and never backward. The most lasting lesson from my family has been the ability to endure the trials of life, knowing I had the strength of my entire family behind me, providing the needed support, encouragement to continue, and always with a prayer coupled with hope.

***

I sit in the comfort of my home in Virginia, exploding with comforts seen on television re-runs, like the Nelson family household or *The Cosby Show*. The house boasts four bedrooms, two family rooms, a den, an office, and a dining room overlooking the turquoise water of a swimming pool. The water reflects the colors of the Gulf waters of Mexico and reminds me of the Gulf waters at the foot of the Mayan Pyramid of Tulum.

However, the swimming pool at my abode lacks the spirituality achieved by the citizens who inhabited the ancient Temple of Tulum. My extravagant surroundings made me realize that my life has become one of over-indulgence. Who needs a ridiculous amount of square footage for only two people? The purchase of such a large home was my overreaction to the fear of being poor. It was my belief that owning such a large home would make me feel like I was never poor. Living in such a large home was my way to announce my arrival into a socio-economic setting that I had pursued and often thought could never be achieved by me or anyone rising from the poverty of farm labor, better known by mainstream America as a migrant farm worker.

The distance between myself and the days of hunger and day-long fieldwork seems like an eternity, worlds apart, and as if I never lived through it. Like it never happened. My dream was to put the distance of time and memory between now and then, but I realize now that my past is woven within my being. Without the tribulations, I would never have ended up in Virginia with more of life's comforts than I needed. I only set out to break away from working in the fields and not to have to live out of cars or the shacks that were used as excuses for homes provided for the migrant farm workers of this country. This inhumane practice continues to this day.

Now that I'm here, sitting in what I call my office, I realize that not many people care that I finally made it out of poverty. The only person that would or should care is me. No matter what happens from this day forward, I know that I have worked myself into a position in life that provides the opportunity to choose what affects the direction I take. Success, for me, now depends on personal choices and not the accumulation of material things such as the latest model of BMW car to drive or the newest in-home entertainment technology.

It has become more important to know the outcomes of what my actions will produce and to know that I am giving back to the community that has nurtured me and provided me with the strength that keeps me going.

My luxurious home, nestled in the center of wealth, knowledge, and power, was purchased as a symbol that I did not give up on the struggle of breaking the cycle of poverty. I did not give up when I felt the pains of hunger clamp down on my stomach until there was nothing but numbness. I did not give up when I felt anger at the injustice I witnessed and was willing to destroy things and hurt people to lash out in revenge. Giving up was not in the cards I had drawn, waiting to be played.

I recall a time when I was about eleven years. I noticed that some people were evenly tanned while others were tanned only where the sun could touch their skin. As a kid, I developed this notion of what being well off meant. Farmers who, to me, were wealthy were always evenly tanned. An even tan was something that could only be achieved if you did not have to protect yourself from being out in the sun all day.

I noticed that when workers took off their hats and scarves or wore long-sleeved shirts, a paler, lighter color of skin appeared in the protected areas. I compared this to the wealthy ranchers or White people in town who were evenly tanned. I remember thinking that when I got rich, I would have a tanned head. This would mean I did not have to wear a hat all day to protect myself from the blistering sun.

Beyond having a complete tan, the most important goal I had as a poor migrant farmworker kid was to be able to eat whenever I got hungry, lay down to rest or sleep when I got tired, and go swimming anytime I wanted, even though I had not learned to swim.

One of the most important personal goals I've achieved is knowing that all I have to do is walk to the kitchen and invade the white fortress that holds my meals for at least a month. The cupboards are also stocked as if they were awaiting a natural disaster and could feed me for an additional month. While I have achieved the goal of erasing traces of poverty and the insecurity it breeds, my spirit has created a stockpile mentality. Some might call it a deprivation mentality. I've been hoarding groceries for the comfort of knowing they are there.

Food was not the only necessity that conditioned my behavior and attitude toward the most basic comforts of life. I no longer have to look for tar paper to tack onto wooden planks covering the cracks between the boards used as walls, sealing the daylight of dusk from sneaking through. This was a common occurrence as we traveled from place to place, working in the farm fields of the rural West.

I'm still overwhelmed with the capacity of the gas furnace that provides heat for my entire house without having to go out and cut wood for the stove. In my youth, the cooking stove doubled as a furnace in our one-room shacks, our temporary homes. Regardless of whether it was night or day, freezing or raining, we ventured to the wood pile for the source of energy that brought us the simple comforts of cooking or providing extra heat.

My arrival to this new world of choices and self-determination allowed me to control the stinging cold that once caused me to shiver in my bed simply by setting a thermostatic control to seventy-five degrees and waiting for a few minutes while the entire house warms up. Today, those comforts are controlled by the flip of a switch. Guilt sets in as I think about those who are still coping with third-world conditions. Why should I have four bedrooms when entire families sleep in one large room with three or four beds crowded together? I recall the living quarters, so close that I could hear my aunts praying the Rosary or my uncle sipping on his last beer before going to sleep.

I no longer eat in a kitchen that serves as the gathering place throughout the day and as a bedroom for the entire family at night. There are times I walk through my home and experience a sense of embarrassment, knowing that I own four bedrooms and use only one. I have been looking for this station in life for many years, but it doesn't seem as important as it was when I was nine years old.

In my childhood, we often drove by homes that looked just like this. Today, it seems much more important to know and understand what is inside a home than what a house looks like.

What matters is the interior. Those farmworker shacks, nestled in the middle of fields of mint, beets, potatoes, and strawberries, were where I absorbed a myriad lessons of nature, curiosity, patience, and, most importantly, love from fellow migrants that gave me the confidence to continue.

It wasn't an easy road. I was able to traverse those early years and land in Virginia due to a daily survival routine. I focused on the prize. It was as if the journey became more important than my original goal. Where and when I became so focused eludes me, as far as my memory goes. At an early age, I developed a notion that I could go anywhere I chose and do anything I set my mind to. This mindset has taken me through diverse worlds as I crossed social and economic boundaries in one lifetime.

None of it would have been possible without the foundation established by my family and a series of friendships that developed throughout my travels. I left friends behind, never to see them again, but they certainly made an indelible mark. In some cases, they recognized my drive and kept me from getting involved in illegal activities. They pointed me away from falling prey or taking the easy route.

One occasion had a major impact on choosing the positive. A close friend, Michael, came from single parent family with a father so absent that we planned drinking parties at his house without any worry of an adult interrupting our reckless celebration. Michael was always fun to be with. He was always laughing and joking and coming up with audacious challenges for us to foolishly take on. On one of those days, when we were sitting around having a few beers, he concocted a scheme to break into a hardware store that he believed to be foolproof. I remember thinking that Mike, as we called him, always came up with wild ass ideas that would inevitably backfire, landing him in a state of constant trouble.

My thinking at the time was that Mike was my friend, and I believed him. As he began laying out his plan, I couldn't help blurting out, "Hey, I want to go!" Mike suddenly stopped explaining his plan and stood up, looked me in the eye, and said, "No, you can't go." He went on to say that I was not like him and that I had another destiny. He told me I belonged in another place. My immediate reaction was, *does he think I belong in another place because I'm Mexican?* Maybe he didn't trust me. At that moment, I did not understand what had happened, and being rejected so suddenly by a good friend stuck with me for the longest time.

While I did not understand it then, I know now that our friendship was more than just an acquaintance. It was a kind of respect and love that comes with a bond of brotherhood. Over time my realization is that my friends saw something different in me that they wanted to protect. They could see I had a chance to make it out. It seemed as if there was a hidden spirit that kept driving me in certain directions. I did not know the destination or the outcome, but the friendships I developed encouraged me to explore beyond familiarity into unknown places. Sometimes, it felt as if my friends intentionally pushed me away to the point that I could see there was no space where I could fit in. I was different but did not know how different.

I've always had that burning desire to know what was over the next hill or beyond the snow-covered mountains. Even today, it's like a terminal disease that keeps spreading, and the longer it's left unattended, the faster it grows until it cannot turn back. Thankfully, the answers to my curious questions have always been within reach.

By following my instincts for survival and my willingness to take risks without fear of the unknown, I managed to escape the ugly jaws of poverty before I knew what I wanted to be. The fear of hunger and the need for shelter is the type of motivator that can nip at your heels, never letting you forget. All I knew was that I seemed destined to make contributions that would return benefits to the community I left behind.

A silent aspiration was to break out of a hand-to-mouth existence, go to college to study art and become wealthy. How to get there was never prescribed, but the notion nestled in my sub-conscience. Over time, it grew into a goal that would change frequently over time.

An intellectual way of describing it is that, on one hand, success is the act of eluding poverty and living comfortably. On the other hand, success can come at a price. In my case, both are true. I am far from impoverished, yet I sacrificed much to get there, including my dreams of raising children. My fear was that I would be left with thoughts of a family that could have been and memories of a service record of paying it forward.

Seeking success has catapulted me through impenetrable socio-economic barriers. I have learned how to compete in a mainstream world that has required me to learn behaviors that are not necessarily suited to my culture or my personality but more suited to the nature of competition and living in America. It has been necessary for me to learn how to stay a Mexican in a culturally foreign land known for pressuring citizens to be melted into the pot of the American way of life.

This melting pot theory has caused young ethnic children confusion in figuring out who they are. The melting pot channels young minds into thinking they should become someone they can never be. I much prefer the viewpoint of former President Jimmy Carter, who said, "We have become not a melting pot but a beautiful mosaic. Different people, different beliefs, different yearnings, different hopes, different dreams." You see, from birth, I was raised as a Mexican in every sense of the word, from speaking Spanish to the Indian healing practices to religion and the strong relationships with my extended family.

Why is it that people from different ethnic and cultural backgrounds who choose to live in this wonderful country we call America, are forced to face the dilemma of denying one culture for another—one that is oftentimes difficult, if not impossible, to define? Isn't it much more valuable for this nation to have citizens expanding their knowledge in more than one language and culture than to spend time and energy trying to get them to forget their native tongues and cultural heritage? What is the logic or the efficiency in learning another language and assimilating another culture, only to be used as a lever that creates a lasting internal conflict for having denied who you were since birth?

Like most new arrivals to this land of opportunity, we gradually, over time, begin to question our origins and struggles about who we are or what we have become. I had to question myself. *Where did I come from?* I know I have ancestors from Mexico and Spain, with most of my heritage stemming from an Indigenous people native to what is now called America. It feels disrespectful to describe an entire community as one group when there could be people from more than two dozen countries spanning the American continent, the Caribbean, and Spain. We do not all come from the same place, and we are not alike.

Confused Assimilation

Lost in society's assimilation, a plan,

Bound by history, in a straitjacket, arms intertwined,

Muscles tightened, striving to escape, subtle signs, bombarded,

Social, economic, political pressures, constant and never-ending,

Demands that I relinquish to an unknown's grip,

insistence to abandon my search,

Struggling to discover self-identity, fighting to reveal the elusive reality,

Pushing, pulling, yanking, breath involuntarily
escaping my lungs on fire,

Suffocating, near the brink of despair, rebellion
stirs, a swift serpent, uncoiling.

Striking at my faltering will, leaving me shaken,
confronting the adversary,

Polished leather shoes, approaching with blind
determination, without reason.

Scuffing their gleaming surface, revealing hidden
causes, unknown agendas.

Unveiling a face marked by mirrored reflections,
fear lurks in the shadows.

Cautious steps moving forward, wisdom,
experience,

ancient spirits guiding me.

Moving from the past into the future, my spirit
clings to our ancestors' foundations.

Concrete monasteries, standing to confuse, yet I
resist abandoning where I have come from,

Driven to where I am meant to be, a battle rages
on, threatening to consume my soul.

This is not the time, and I will not relinquish.

CHAPTER 3
Memories of Matriarchs

Una tía es una amiga, una confidente y una segunda madre, todo en uno.
(An aunt is a friend, a confidante, and a second mother, all in one.)
~ Author Unknown

This is a good place to talk about those who surrounded me in childhood. Even today, the sound of tin cups and platters rattle echoes of a world that seemed like a dream without meaning, people talking of things unknown to me.

For all intents and purposes, my aunts became my mother. A maternal mystery lingered because my mother was absent. Why? I didn't know. I only had the vaguest memories of her which I explain later in the book, and oddly my life was so enveloped with love that I didn't miss her, at least not consciously.

Growing up on Cherry Street in Eagle Pass was an experience that would be difficult to replicate today. We were fortunate to be able to have family on either side of our home and be able to walk down the street and around the corner and still be in our family neighborhood. As an extended family, we enjoyed playing, praying, and working together. Along with my immediate aunts and uncles, it was my extended family that would be part of our journeys north. It was as if our small neighborhood was loaded and transported on the trip north for the families' livelihood.

I was a little boy who managed to cope quite well thanks to my grandparents and my aunts. I was born in 1949 in Eagle Pass, Texas, right across the U.S.-Mexico border and given the Spanish-Christian name of Victor. At an early age, my brother and I were sent to live with my grandparents because we were too young to travel with the caravan with our extended family as they traveled north from one farm to another. My grandparent's home was a humble adobe house in Piedras Negras, Mexico. The house had a dirt floor that was sprinkled with water every morning and then swept and cleaned so smoothly that it had the texture of fine cement. I can still recall the musty, sweet smell of water touching clay, then drying to a pale gray from the heat of the Mexican sun, filled the house and my memories.

In the center of the backyard was an altar where the family worshipped, a spot where fires were lit for evening gatherings. The rising flames called the household to meet. Our tradition was to discuss the activities of the day and listen as elders told and retold ancient stories.

The evening gatherings were a time to share troubles and joys, a place where laughter followed even the most serious of predicaments. Laughter was always the easiest. It provided the greatest relief. After all, as my abuela would say, "Why worry about those things over which we have no control? God always shows us the way if we have the faith to be led." Wise words from a wise woman. We sat and watched the fire until the spirits in the dark began to force our eyes shut. Then we headed to the kitchen and fell, exhausted on our mats and bedrolls, all collectively falling to sleep in this small space.

The morning soon sneaked into our dreams and woke us with the help of a rooster bugling that the creeping sun was violating his perch. In the semi-darkness of the early morning, my grandmother began her day by gathering wood for the black iron wood stove sitting in the corner of the small kitchen, now bustling with activity. We were reminded by the sunlight revealing itself through one small window that it was time to get ready for work. Once the fire got going, my grandmother pumped the handle of the water pump over the sink to draw water, which she boiled to make coffee in a beat-up tin pot. She poured the coffee grounds right into the pot. As the brew began to percolate, the aroma energized the household, filling it (and us) with an aroma that pinched my nose, arousing my senses into a light hunger.

I knew it would soon be time for a morning walk to the neighborhood bakery. My older brother Gerardo and I usually followed my grandfather down the street, greeting neighbors who were out watering down sidewalks and sweeping them clean from yesterday's activity. Out came the fruit and vegetable vendors and the workers leaving their homes for the sugarcane fields or the factory. There was always time for a quick smile, a hello, and sometimes a few moments to talk about the day to come, with the discussion usually focused on work.

We made this daily walk to buy a variety of pan dulce, but my all-time favorite was a type of gingerbread shaped like a little pig called cochinitos. If they were more than a day old, their freshness could be revived by soaking them in coffee for the slightest moment, but if they soaked too long, they became soggy and broke into inedible pieces. Selecting the right bread for the morning feast was crucial to please my grandmother's taste buds. She anxiously waited once the table was set with coffee and leche Pet (canned condensed Pet Milk) for the adults, goat's milk with sugar added for the children, accompanied by a sweet roll for the first meal (a snack, really) at 5:30 a.m. We all sat at the table while my grandmother strained the coffee through cheesecloth. Once ready, it was poured into blue tin cups with black speckled spots except for a couple of cups with round black dots where the blue porcelain had been chipped away.

My abuelita poured coffee for my abuelo and then for Gerardo, my oldest brother, and then for me, being the youngest male at the table. She served herself last. Goat's milk and sugar are flavors I've never been able to duplicate. Maybe it was that the goat's milk was so fresh it was still warm for the goat, or the coffee, ground so fine that is had to be strained through cheesecloth. To this day, my morning coffee reminds me that true wealth comes from the simplicity of family rituals, love, and the basics, such as coffee, a sweet roll, and family sitting together and sharing plans for the day.

This simple life was splendid. I listened to my abuela reminding my abuelo of what he needed to do that day. When we finished eating and he had his daily instructions, my abuelo was ready to go to the cane fields. In a few hours, he'd come back for another breakfast because the energy of the early morning coffee and roll would be gone.

Traveling to the cane fields was always an adventure. My brother and I rode in the back of a wooden cart pulled by a single burro that had memorized our destination. My abuelo didn't have to urge the burro in any direction. The burro just started walking as soon as we were on board, and it followed the dirt roads leading to the field that would be cut that day. My brother and I spent the mornings playing in the section of the field that had already been cut and where the cane had been hauled to the mercado.

During the day, we made routine trips back and forth, hauling the cut sugar cane to the house to take to the market. I always looked forward to the end of the day because my grandfather took a stalk of cane and stripped it for my brother and me. We peeled back the skin and chewed as we rode back on a bed of moist green cane with its sweet honey smell.

The taste of fresh-cut sugar cane has never left my taste buds. When I chew a stalk, I'm back on the wooden cart drawn by the short brown burro with the warm sun on my back. It brings back a sense of comfort because I know that I was happy. I had no sense of poverty or deprivation. I felt as if I had everything. Oh, to capture those feelings forever.

***

My brother Gerado and I grew up with our grandparents, surrounded by love and mystery. From our earliest memories, we didn't understand why our parents weren't together or why our father was away, working in a place where children couldn't go. All we knew was that he was far away, and I often wished I could grow up faster so I could join him.

The reason for my parents' separation was never spoken of in our family, but a childhood memory remained vivid in my mind. I was just learning to walk when one night; my father came into the labor shack where we lived and found my mother with another man from the camp. I remember the anger on his face and the black pistol he pulled from behind his back, pointing it at my mother.

I didn't understand what was happening, but I felt an instinctive fear of the gun and a need to protect my mother. I climbed onto a hundred-pound sack of pinto beans, struggling to stand up and meet my father's gaze. As I reached out, he laid the pistol down on the kitchen counter, tears streaming down his sun-tanned cheeks. That image of my father, vulnerable and broken, remained with me to this day.

It wasn't until I was older that I understood the significance of that night and why we moved to live with our grandparents. The silence of my mother in our family was profound, yet no one ever spoke ill of her. My grandmother and aunts filled the void of her absence, and I grew up with a neutral sense of who she was, shaped by the quiet strength of the women around me.

One late summer afternoon, when the harvest of sugar cane was completed, my father, Victoriano, pulled up in front of my grandparents' house in a blue '56 Ford. My father drove on a dirt road and should only have been passable by mountain goats and came for us. I didn't miss him until I saw him walking toward me with his arms open, waiting to catch me as I ran and jumped into them. There was joy and sadness in this reunion.

My father had come to take us to live with the rest of the family. We had reached an age when we could begin traveling with the rest of the family. At the time I did not understand how old they were and that my grandparents' health was failing. It was time to transport my brother and me to a new home that, thankfully, we were already familiar with. We were headed to my aunts—my wonderful, kind, wise, and loving aunts. And once again, I realized that I had a father, but there was no one that I could recognize or miss as my mother. Again, it was a blessing to have mother surrogates who loved me so much, but the small seed of confusion and questioning was never quite squashed.

So, my father's coming would soon unite me and my brother with the rest of the family, specifically our other siblings. While Gerardo and I were living with our abuelos, who had become our parents, our sisters, Idelia and Lenor, lived with two aunts in Eagle Pass, Texas, surrounded by six other family households.

As we drove away from my abuelos' humble home, I didn't realize I'd never see them again. To me, they were immortal caregivers, old, wise, and giving. They provided everything an inquisitive little boy could hope for in a countryside village. But I was destined to live in el otro lado (the other side or in the U.S.)—Eagle Pass, a primarily Mexican American community. Even Eagle Pass would not be my permanent home because we were destined to move from one community to another with the rest of my family as we followed the crop harvests and worked for six to eight months each year to earn enough to get the family through the winter. My family worked the land like the ancient Indians, planting and harvesting for the future.

Once we moved into our new neighborhood surrounded by family, it didn't take long for me to figure out how convenient it would be to walk up and down the street and try to decide which of my cousins I wanted to play with or where I might want to have breakfast, lunch or dinner. My days on Cherry

Street were spent going from house to house, playing games with my cousins, and visiting my aunts and uncles. It seems that no matter what home I went into, it always felt like walking into my own home. There would always be a cousin, aunt, or uncle to greet me at the screen door, shouting at me to come in, and the first words would be, "Are you hungry? "Have you had anything to eat?" "Let me make you a little taco before you go."

Growing up on Cherry Street in Eagle Pass was an experience that would be difficult to replicate today. As an extended family, we enjoyed playing, praying, and working together. Along with my immediate aunts and uncles, it was my extended family that would be part of our journey north. It was as if our small neighborhood was loaded and transported on the trip north for the families' livelihood.

The Tias

In an endless list of people to thank in my early years, aside from my grandparents, my tias (Aunts) are at the top. They tended to my well-being, and I very much appreciate Tias Carmen, Ricarda (Rico), Guadalupe (Lupe), and Concepcion (Concha) for their love and care.

When I began this book, Tia Carmen, the eldest of three sisters on my father's side, had passed on to the next world. She held on until all her children, including her nieces and nephews, reached their "place of comfort," meaning happy and purposeful lives. Tia Carmen was the foundation that supported the structure that we called home, she was the roof that protected us from the unexpected and the one that pointed us to the doorways that offered opportunity. Tia Carmen was not only the foundation supporting the house she was also the one who had a gift to heal. I recall when my youngest brother Ricardo (Rick who was twenty years younger than me.) who was T-boned by another car while driving home totaling the vehicle he was driving and for some miraculous reason escaped physical injury but was so traumatized that he was afraid to get into a vehicle. After weeks of trying to coax my brother to get into a vehicle and shake the trauma my father suggested that he should go visit my Tia Carmen.

After weeks of gentle prodding, Rick finally decided to call my aunt for help. She agreed to perform a cleansing and set the appointment for seven o'clock the next morning. When Rick arrived, only my aunt was home, and we weren't allowed to accompany him inside. We left at seven in the morning and didn't receive a call to pick him up until ten-thirty that evening.

When we arrived, Rick appeared from the house, walking toward our car with a newfound strength and positivity. He got into the car without a word about what had happened during the healing session. As we drove home, the silence was filled with a palpable sense of relief; Rick was no longer afraid to get into a vehicle. Though that day has never been discussed since, we knew he had been freed from his trauma. Tía Carmen truly had a special gift.

When my Tia Carmen married, my Tia Rico, the second sister, became the head of the family at age fourteen after my grandparents died. She raised two generations of children—her seven siblings and their children. I looked to Tia Rico as the one I could count on to tell me about life in general, who to trust or not, how to learn from my mistakes, and most importantly, how to use my creative energy in a positive way. With Tia Rico I could do no wrong. Tia Lupe (short for Guadalupe), the third sister, the soft-spoken one, helped soothe the pain I experienced in childhood. She would encourage me to be kind and to have an open heart, even toward those who expressed hatred toward me. She always reminded me to make sure that I married a Mexican girl. Tia Concha, my aunt by marriage to my Uncle Frank, taught me to be macho (the old meaning of what macho used to mean) in all the right ways. She taught me the importance of learning to be strong for the family, to take care of my community, and to never forget where I came from.

Of all the homes on our street, the one I favored most was

my uncle José's, Tia Carmen's husband. They were the eldest of the family and always wanted to know what I was doing, how I was feeling, or where I was going. My uncle José was the best cook of all our family members; he learned to cook on a cattle ranch, which often meant cooking over a campfire. Of all the things that he could cook, his cakes baked on the skillet were the best I have ever had. José was a quiet man and never spoke of his time in the Army, but I found out from my father that he was at Normandy on D-Day. I have learned since that it was a miracle that he returned. Besides his excellent cooking skills, I remember that he could roll a Bull Durham cigarette with one hand.

The Christmas holidays were the most enjoyable of all holidays. It was a time when everyone was back from being up north and all gathered in the same neighborhood to celebrate the season as one giant family. There was always a house preparing tamales for Christmas day and each household set a date when people came over and we all made tamales, taking turns, and going from home to home to deliver this delicious food.

On Christmas Eve, everyone dressed up in their best clothes to go to midnight mass and give thanks to all that we have received and ask for blessings for others that were not so fortunate. After mass, each family returned home and began preparing the Christmas meal that would include homemade tamales, of course, and rice and beans. At some point in the early morning, we cooked bunelos, and their aroma on the stove filled the entire neighborhood. It did not matter where on Cherry Street you lived; you knew that when mass was over, we would feast, and our family would begin to cook bunelos all over again.

Eventually, winter ended, and we saw the first hint of spring. Family members began reaching out to each other, visiting and ready to talk about when we would head north and where we would go first. We came together to make family decisions about specific dates and plans and which family oversaw which tasks. Usually, at least five families traveled north as a caravan. Tio Francisco (Pancho is what everyone called him) owned a big truck that all the families used to transport basic household items such as pots, pans, bedding, and extra clothing for work and various weather conditions.

Their presence constantly reinforced the notion that children who have any hope of realizing their dreams can only keep that hope with the help of their families and the entire community. My relatives also handed down the time-honored belief systems of our people. Guidance and early lessons came in the form of ancient Indian stories. Later, I would call them campfire stories, where I sat in wonderment as my family spoke of the old ways.

But for now, I was living in a loving home amid these loving souls. Thank heavens, for I sorely needed them. Once, I laid on my sick bed with my Tia Rico taking care of me. And now, in hindsight, I realize she did all she could to save my young life.

Tia Rico recalled this harrowing story several times over the years, and looking back, it's a miracle I didn't die. I had a swollen face and was unable to shake loose a high fever for what we believed was the mumps. No one in the family could figure out what was wrong with me, and they could not afford to go to the doctor so natural healing was the course of action. No matter what remedies they tried, the fever persisted. I remember the heat of it surrounding my features and boiling to the tips of my ears down to the meaty part of my legs. I felt weak to the point that I couldn't even laugh.

Eventually, Tia Rico decided to call the local curandera (natural healer) from Piedras Negras. And thus, a woman who was new to my world healed me. She also cast a prediction about how my life would turn out, which, indeed, came true.

There are distinct types of curanderos, there are ones for healing and others who cast evil spells. Good health, prosperity, and love can be received from healers, and these positive attributes can be taken away quickly through a simple ritual practiced by curanderos or curanderas. These healers were common in our community, with the ancient secrets of healing and the skill to practice natural healing. They have always lived among us from the beginning of time into the present, and more than likely, they will have a presence in our future.

Our healers did not go to formal schools or receive the type of training that we are familiar with. Instead, curanderos are often born into an art passed down from family member to family member. The degree of knowledge that a curandero depends on what they were taught by an elder, who typically relied on memories of what had been passed down and limited by the recurrence of individual memories of what had been taught and what was allowed to be revealed. It may be that memory controls the healers themselves.

Curanderos resisted the introduction of Christianity. It is common to observe superstitious beliefs linked to natural healers blended into Christian beliefs to make sure that none of the gods would be insulted. For example, the serpent can be found painted along the bottom of the Virgin de Guadalupe's robe, and food can be found at the foot of statues of saints. The beliefs are so deeply ingrained that in our household, we slept with water glasses next to our beds so the evil spirits would have something to drink when they were thirsty and leave us alone.

As I lay in my sick bed, a curandera came to our home to cure me of the fever. Her name was never spoken to me or anyone in the room. She at once caught my eye as she walked into the room and stared into my soul. It seemed as if we had known each other from some other place in time. Even though she was old and ugly, covered with wrinkles baked dry by the sun, she made me feel at ease with her touch. Her eyes never left my sight. She began her healing by lighting incense on a porcelain plate, pushing smoke in my face, and covering my body with scented incense. Then she began rubbing the shell of a raw, unbroken egg all over my body, concentrating mostly around my chest.

Then suddenly, she broke the egg into a small bowl that lay at the foot of the bed. I watched as she studied the contents. She looked at my father and Tia Rico and spoke softly to them, pointing to the egg. She said it had spots of blood, so the red blotchy spot on my neck, the fever, and the mumps-like symptoms meant someone was giving me "el ojo," the evil eye.

This pronouncement gave me a scare like I had never felt before. How could anyone get rid of the evil eye once they got it? La curandera sensed my fear because almost as soon as I began to panic, she reached over to me and began to caress my chest like you would a young puppy that gets a little too excited as she stared into my eyes, she said, "Mijo, you don't have anything to worry about. You are going to get better. You will grow to old age, become well educated, fight for your people, and be wealthy. You will become famous because of your work."

The fear disappeared as she prepared a concoction of fried banana peel with special herbs, powders, and liquids that she had brought with her. This was done in a large skillet on our wood stove. Once the remedy had been prepared, she spread the paste on my cheeks, neck, and upper body. The remedy was blended into a paste that was spread all over my body. Who knows if this truly did me any good or not, but I believe it did. It didn't matter because within three days I was healed of my illness and given access to a foreseen destiny.

While it may not seem odd to be listening to some sort of fortuneteller, it was rather odd to believe her explicitly. But there was no reason for me to question her. After all, she made me feel better by healing me from the pain of the fever. She cured me of the illness that kept me confined and in bed. Questioning her knowledge or motivation was not something that I or any members of my family were prepared to do. She carried with her a power that even the Catholic priests did not have. This curandera was protected by the ancient secrets of her healing power as well as her knowledge of Christian ways. She had managed to capture the strength of both powers.

My recollection of this old woman is vivid, a picture that is carried in my memory that can be recalled upon request. This old woman created the possibility and the hope that had not been there until she suggested it. How daring to think of being a college professor and artist or, God forbid, a writer. The curandera was a dream maker in a young boy's mind. She brings tears to the very fiber of my being just knowing that one human being can touch another in passing moments, touching a soul in a way that lasts a lifetime.

You see, I have always felt I was spared for a reason. And true to the curandera's words, which all came true, I survived to absorb more lessons from my elders, as described in the adventures ahead.

CHAPTER 4
Mis Tios

La familia no es sólo quienes son de tu sangre, sino son los que nunca nos abandonan.
(Family is not only those who are of your blood but are those who never leave us.)
~Dicho

Tio Jose was always my favorite uncle beyond his cooking skills, he could bake the most delicious cakes from scratch in a skillet over a campfire. He always had time to listen to any story we wanted to share. Tio Jose always seemed to have time to blend a bit of wisdom in his responses. Jose was a quiet man who didn't drink, but chain smoked his trademark cigarette, Bull Durham, which came in a soft cotton pouch full of tobacco that closed by pulling strings together. He smoked so much that he perfected the art of sprinkling the fine tobacco on cigarette paper, which he rolled with one hand as he carried on conversations with the rest of the family.

Each of my aunt's and uncles' homes had similar decorations. It did not matter which family home I walked into there was always a picture of Jesus, usually in a principal place, with a picture of the Virgin de Guadalupe somewhere nearby and one of President Kennedy. Candles were always placed next to a saint's picture, and sometimes they were lit for a special request or prayers for a person or purpose. Along with these pictures declaring our Catholicism were pictures of family members and pictures of those who had served in the military, thus proclaiming the family's loyalty to the United States, a home that had given us so much.

Most of my uncles—Jose, Geronimo, Juan, and my father—all served during World War II. Tio Jose was a quiet man and survivor of the invasion of Normandy Beach. He never spoke of his time in the military, but deep down, I know that something haunted him. We lost one uncle (Roberto) on D-Day as America made its way into Europe, even though no one knew much about the war except that we had to provide warriors from our community to serve and protect. There is no fear of dying when you have nothing to lose, and you know that you will return to this earth to experience another life. I have always carried the uncle that I never knew in my heart, and I understood who he was even though he died before I was born. He made the ultimate sacrifice in a place he had never seen or knew about. He may have returned as one of my closest friends if not for this tragedy.

None of my uncles ever spoke of any wartime exploits, although they knew other veterans in Eagle Pass and always supported each other when there was a need. From my uncles who served in the military and experienced the travesty of war, I learned to listen to the silence of those who have lived through the conflicts, and the trauma created by war. These were the uncles that served as my role models at home and when we migrated north for work.

Our Caravans north always looked at Oregon as a place to drive through and a place to occasionally stop to earn some quick money for food and gas for the next big job, which would usually be in Washington State, beginning in the Yakima Valley. Short stops in Oregon would last anywhere from a few days to a couple of weeks, the time used to send someone ahead to find work for everyone that would last more than a week. On one occasion, Tio Flaco who was a distant cousin heard that they were looking for veterans to work at the Umatilla Army Depot during one of these scouting trips to the Tri-Cities area of Washington (Kennewick, Pasco, and Richland).

While my father and uncles were farm workers, they were all veterans. My father served in the Pacific theater for the duration of the war, while two of his brothers served in Europe.

I grew up believing that it was my duty to serve in the United States military regardless of any personal cost to me. While there was never any pressure for me to join the military, I always felt an unwritten understanding that when the time came, I would volunteer to do my duty.

The holidays from November through January were a time for family to be together before our yearly migration. I recall chatter about when we would leave, who was going, who would stay, and always the inevitable debate of where we would be going. As the end of February and early March approached, the family meetings began to spontaneously erupt in preparations. Even though we discussed going to many distinct parts of the U.S., we could only agree on what we had done before. We never migrated beyond what we knew.

Over the years, our family learned which farmers paid on time, kept their word, and, in some cases, which farms provided housing. Our travels began in Eagle Pass, heading west to California and then into Oregon, Washington, Idaho, and Utah. Sometimes, on rare occasions, we would spend a few weeks in New Mexico. During the winters, we returned to our homes in Texas.

Livelihood

The beets are planted,

Ready, growing green blades, awakening.

People are sleeping, winter's end approaching.

Praying in the snow, waiting for a bountiful

harvest

Frost on their lips, sun rising easing the
numbness,

Purple and swollen.

It is time, looking north, chewing on week-old
tortillas, no more food, time to work.

Asking for a raise would be rude. We need the
money.

Thoughts of our ancestors, who was here before?

Survival continues, dignity stolen for wages, food,
shelter, and a trip home.

Their legacy born in a beet field, future in
accumulating knowledge.

Knowledge preserved, revived, taught, and passed
on.

My uncles and their families would get together and discuss the best way to find farms that offered opportunities. Everything had to be planned out to make every move count and maximize our abilities with the least amount of downtime. Any days off meant we would earn less money to bring home for the winter in Texas. Going north meant we could take only a few of our things on the trip. We would be in any given place a month at a time, and on rare occasions, we might spend a couple of months in a temporary shelter.

In preparation for the four-day trip, a menu of foods that would tolerate four days of exposure to overwhelming heat during the day and the sudden cooling in the starlit nights in the desert. Our menu included a variety of foods that ranged from tamales that were usually the first to go, bean and egg tacos with homemade flour tortillas and a lot of hard-boiled eggs that seemed to last longer than most foods.

After the cooking for the trip was done, we started packing the truck with our personal belongings: clothes, pots and pans, and some small pieces of furniture. Everyone was allowed some space on the truck. Once the truck was loaded, there was still a little room in the cars. Three or four cars with six to seven people followed the truck. The caravan was ready except for loading the prepared food: burritos, boiled eggs, and sometimes plain tortillas. We also took raw potatoes wrapped in aluminum foil to cook on the car's engine manifold as we traveled down the road occasionally stopping to turn the potatoes or poke in a fork and see if they were cooked.

After an hour or so, we pulled over and turned the potato over so they would "bake" evenly. We always had some baked potatoes available for anyone who wanted one. We warmed our tacos and burritos in the same way on the manifold next to the potatoes.

The routine was to go through California first to pick strawberries. Early in the harvest season, it was the berry crops that we searched out: strawberries to raspberries. As summer approached, we looked for work further north, often in Washington State, where we hoed mint plants, beets, or picked potatoes. Sometimes, when we were lucky, we worked in the hop fields. The hop growers normally had better housing, meaning individual units that could accommodate families.

Our journey north typically included three to four families from my father's side of the family, along with other families from the community. We would travel in caravans like many families had done before us. Many people who had migrated before us became the early settlers in California, Oregon, Washington, and Idaho. Little did I know that we were retracing the migrating path back to the ancient lands that at one time had been part of the ancient migratory path that led us south and later became the northernmost territory of Mexico all the way to the Yucatan and Central America.

Most of the families traveled with husbands, wives, children, aunts, uncles, and cousins, so housing was a huge consideration. Farmworker housing was typically basic. More often than not, it was one large open space with a wood stove, furnished with a couple of dusty gray stained mattresses mounted on a steel framed bed with springs that provided a bounce when you sat on it. No indoor plumbing existed, which meant there was no water for washing, cooking, or drinking. We brought every drop of water from a faucet typically installed in an outbuilding intended for cleaning the equipment. A community outhouse was at one end of the complex, and community showers were available in a separate building or sometimes a barn or workshop.

When I was young, I was bathed by my aunts, who used the tubs for washing and rinsing our clothes and on washday as a bathtub. They were so huge they seemed like swimming pools. My aunts and the other women's showers would be separate from the men's but usually set up in the same vicinity, so we had to take turns. The girls, women, and babies showered first. Then, it was our turn.

As my brother Gerardo and I got older, we graduated to the showers with the men. We cleaned ourselves in the makeshift showers installed on an overhead beam with the water supplied by a hose from the outbuilding faucet. A hot shower was only a fantasy, and I would not experience a hot shower until we returned to Texas. I remember taking a shower with the men for the first time, and I thought it was odd that my uncles had hair on parts of their bodies when I had none. *How could that be?* I wondered. It seemed disgusting at the time. But the mysteries of puberty and adulthood would eventually catch up with me as I later morphed into an anatomical version of the men in the showers.

As we waited to shower, we worked at sharpening our hoes for the next day's work. Without a sharp hoe, you would use up more energy attacking the weeds, and in most instances, they would defeat you by blistering your hands bloody until you took time out to sharpen them. I knew my hoe was sharp enough when it could shave the hair off the back of my arm. That was always the test. My hoe had been cut down to fit my size, and everyone knew it was mine. I felt proud to know that the rest of the family recognized me as someone who worked and contributed.

***

The number of times we moved would not be decided by the farmers and ranchers who needed workers. Instead, the decisions hinged on the crop and whether it was paid by the hour, by the acre, or through a contractor. Our family leaned toward getting paid by the acre because we could manage what got done and how long it would take without the interference of bosses or contractors. Another consideration was the length of the harvest. The longer we stayed in one place, the more the families could save for the winter.

Planning trips and traveling to unfamiliar places always seemed like an adventure with many surprises. We never knew where we would end up or what families we'd meet that we hadn't seen in a year. I was anxious to see old friends and especially a family of boys that were given the nickname of Los Changos, or the monkey boys by people from our community. I always hoped they would arrive at the same camps. We played a game of drawing circles in the light brown dirt and then stomping our feet. The dirt exploded out from under our shoes, fine like talcum powder. If you waited for just the right moment, you could spray dirt all over the person standing next to you.

This was also a time when we got together with family members from other parts of Texas, a sort of family reunion. Catching up with cousins from Brownsville, Corpus Christi, and El Paso became a yearly ritual in the camps of the Yakima

Valley, usually in Sunnyside, Mabton, or Grandview in Washington state.

Finally, the day came for us to begin our journey down the many highways that had become familiar by sight. We drove past many landmarks that I came to recognize. Driving through Alpine and north to El Paso and finally out of Texas, I knew which highways would be next and where there were rest areas that could be used as picnic stops. The whole caravan stopped, and sometimes new families joined us. Tias Lupe and Rico took charge as usual and directed the setting up of the picnic site, unpacking the food, and refilling the burlap bags that were our source of water. They hung from the bumpers or rear-view mirrors of each vehicle in case of emergency and to quench our thirst when crossing the desert.

As we continued our expedition, the new towns along the highways did not always welcome caravans of what the Anglos called "migrant" and "seasonal" farm workers. On one of the trips north, I stood in a field and realized that as happy as I was with my family, there were things surrounding us that were not fair or open because of who we were, the language we spoke, and the color of our skin. On one of these hot, humid days, I began to question why, what is it that we do that causes people to dislike us so much.

During summertime, the weeds grew at such a rapid pace that a field that we had cleared two days prior would begin to challenge the mint plants in a battle for survival all over again. The smell was sweet and always reminded me of Vicks Vapo, the medicine that was put on my chest whenever I had a small cough (a torture for a young child). My aunts believed that Vicks could cure anything. They would put Vicks on the bottom part of our nostrils or on our feet. We had no way of knowing where this healing concoction would be placed to fend off even the slightest ailment.

***

My job in the mint fields was to hoe weeds away from the mint plants, separating them from each other with the resistance of a couple separating to get a divorce. I was nine and had few priorities, but one was owning and riding a bike or going swimming, things important to a young boy's life. Working in the fields was something I didn't think much about. It was what we did—my father, brother, sisters, aunts, and uncles all worked together. Our daily goal was to focus on finishing weeding the entire field and earn the money we needed to save for winter. While I remained focused on my work, I recall hearing young children playing off in the distance. The sounds of their laughter echoed through the bodegas (warehouses) that were always close to the labor camps where the adults too old to work would watch the very youngest children. On one day we were trying to clear thirty acres of weeds by the end of the day as it would mean that everyone would get paid for this contract, and we could start another field. The added prize was a more comfortable winter in Eagle Pass, home to most of the people in the field with us from the Cherry Street neighborhood.

Under an Aztec Sun

I was born in a lettuce field.

Playing in a labor camp

Dust on my breath

As the eagle passed

To the north, we traveled in caravans.

Sweat, salty-sweet sweat.

Rounding my lips

The earth cracked.

Clenching the sweat from our bodies

Ancestors chasing shadows.

Lost children laughing

Watching the Eagle Pass

My spirit flew alongside the eagle.

Wing tip snapping one on one.

As you handed me your heart

You gave me your eagle's flight with love.

Your courage to struggle

The sun in my soul

You taught me to believe in silent men.

Voices glaring from their eyes.

You taught me pride of our new culture.

New history and new pyramids

Faith of the past blended into the future

I chased the eagle to new horizons.

Perching at the beginning of history

Pilgrims arriving in our world.

A new world of visitors

Building stick houses, brightly colored automobiles

Arriving all over the world of Atzlan

We began talking in different tongues.

Understanding one, hiding another

All thirsty for knowledge

Of the unturned page

You gave me friends in the forum.

You gave me the will to fly.

Where the eagle passes to the North

You gave me a chance to understand.

Why you love this country?

This I will give to you, Dad!

With your wisdom and Love

I am a Mejicano of Atzlan.

As the day progressed and people worked at their own pace, they began to separate, off in the distance, I could see small figures marching through the mint fields in the methodical fashion of an army battalion on a seek-and-destroy mission. Bright-colored heads of reds, blues, and browns wore bandanas or hats for protection from the sun with no mercy. Within moments, sweat would dry into our clothes, stained by each hour spent clearing the thirty acres. As heat waves rose, distant chatter blended into an ancestral chant, a prayer to the Sun God to be merciful to those harvesting its bounty. The sun grew closer as the morning coolness wore off, and we began to shed our protection from the morning chill. Hunger began to set in, and I knew that after lunch the true test of my endurance and my ability to contribute would be tested. I wanted so badly to contribute my wages to the family like everyone else.

As a young boy I believed that if I could work until lunchtime that I would pass the test of my transition from childhood to manhood, or at least that was my thinking. After all, as a young man, I would be required to support part of the family, which included going into environmental combat battling the uncontrollable weeds and the searing heat from the afternoon sun and not giving in to childish ideas of playing in the water at the nearby canal. If I could make it to lunchtime, I would be rewarded with cherry Kool-Aid chilled in a gallon pickle jar that had long abandoned its sour contents and welcomed this life-giving fluid. Burritos filled with a great surprise would be on the midday menu, a feast prepared for royalty. The thought of cooling myself with drink and biting into the spicy delights kept me going and allowed me to ignore the pain that gradually began to grow around my fingertips and the palms of my hands.

Lunch was like a family reunion. All my closest relatives were there, including a great uncle who had managed to outlive everyone despite illness, disaster, and the brutality of a revolution. His destiny was to watch his family go through the metamorphosis from one culture to another, which later I would come to realize was an incomplete experiment. It was frequent practice for the entire group to identify the gathering spot for lunch which normally provided shade under the largest nearby tree. When there was no immediate shade, someone would position the largest vehicle as shade for our daily picnic.

There was always time for laughter, joking, or making plans for the future, and to decide where we would go next once this job was done. Decisions on where to go next would be made based on which farmer would pay on time and treat us with respect? Getting paid the right amount without being cheated out of our wages was always unpredictable. We usually had problems with the large corporate farms that used contractors to hire the workers. We did our best to build relationships with small family farms where there was always mutual respect. We admired what the farmer had accomplished. After all, living off the land had been a part of our lives from ancient Aztlán to our struggle in America. I generally felt the farmers respected our hard work and loyalty to their farms, and they could see that we returned year after year.

Eventually our lunch gatherings would end, and the time came to think of attacking the mint field again. We knew that when the morning bird songs faded that the cool of the morning air would go away. The afternoon brought suffocating heat. I could see the heat waves rising from the field, spreading across the horizon until it covered the valley and looked like a mirage, as if a lake was just down the road and we could run there to jump in and cool off. The laughter became less frequent, and the older ones began to talk in a more subdued way, shifting from plans to go to a weekend dance to the repairs the Chevy needed before we went to the next job in Yakima.

My aunts were always the first to rise from lunch, the leaders of the troop. Tia Rico, the matriarch, had everything planned out and gave orders like a well-trained general, but always in a way that had us coming back for more tasks like young pups fetching a stick. Everyone began to move about, knowing exactly what to do and where everything should be placed as they packed the vehicles for the end of the day. My temporary joy of being with everyone in my family was ending. Thoughts of facing that punishing heat began to sneak in and break those moments of laughter.

Tio Flaco was usually the first to step away from the protection of the umbrella-shaped tree that had been protecting us during our meal. He stepped out into a row of mint plants that he intended to save from the wild weeds, intent on rescuing the sweet mint smell that smothered the countryside. Everyone stood up and began moving toward their designated row as if in a trance. I knew it was time to go back into the field, but pain had set in, and I really didn't want to go.

The pressure of everyone at work finally forced me to abandon my fantasies of climbing the tree that served as our guardian. As I walked onto the field and away from the shade, the midday heat pushed against my clothing, and it felt like I was carrying an extra twenty pounds. I could feel the heat entering my body with every breath, and it didn't really matter if I breathed through my mouth or through my nose—my throat immediately began to dry.

Finally, I started hoeing my new row and the soreness began to wear off as my body was gradually reintroduced to the feel of wood, leather, and nine-year-old flesh meeting again. My leather gloves were not from the same family. They had been abandoned by an earlier owner and adopted by me. The hoe I used was my personal possession, given to me by Tio Pancho with strict orders that If I were to have my own hoe, it would be my responsibility to keep it sharpened. A dull hoe would only create more work and give birth to more blisters and more sore muscles.

Not long after I started hoeing, I noticed a young boy coming down the road toward me on a beautiful blue bicycle. As the boy came closer, I could see that he was about my age, and it even seemed that we could be friends without knowing each other. On the back of his bicycle, a snow-white towel was clamped to the back fender. I realized that he was going to the swimming pool. The realization was so stark that I could smell the chlorine and hear the laughter of other children splashing and screaming with joy. It was at this moment I realized that something was wrong. I had to work, and that kid who could have been my friend didn't. In fact, his job was to play like a little kid. He didn't have to be a man.

That young boy on a blue bicycle changed my life and forced me to focus on what I did not want to do. At that moment I realized that I did not want to work on farms all my life. I didn't, however, know for sure what it was I wanted to do.

From that day forward, I knew one thing for sure and it was that I wanted to be able to go swimming anytime I wanted. Something inside me realized there was an easier, better way to live. I became aware of the world outside of the people I loved that day. I didn't know how I would change my life, but I knew it would somehow, someway happen.

El Campo

Arms reaching to the sky.

Razor sharp fingers

Cutting slicing

Searching

An owl with glass eyes

Reaching its destination by memory

Recalling memories

Joy, pain, and hope

The search goes on.

Arms stretching into the sky.

Fingers blunted.

Cutting and slicing

Each fruit an experience

A memory

Each experience, memories

Inches of growth.

Search, experience, growth is fragile.

Breakable through fear

Of being halted prematurely

Its cycle must be complete.

The cycle of a butterfly is complete.

A Monument of Life erected

A mestizo is born.

Symbol of truth

Searching, memory, experience

Returning to the beginning

The ancient lands of Aztlán.

CHAPTER 5
Mi Padre

I was once asked by a reporter why as a non-citizen of the United States, I volunteered to join the military and serve in Vietnam. I answered, 'I was always an American in my heart.

~ Alfredo Velazquez Rascon, Medal of honor recipient

My father was deployed to the Pacific and served for the duration of World War II. A generation later, at eighteen years old, I volunteered to serve and process into the military at Fort Lewis, Washington. Little did I know that I would be taking the same path as my father twenty-six years earlier. I recall waiting in the endless lines of young men from around the country to get a haircut, their uniforms, boots, packs, and all the essentials we would need to become soldiers. In one of the endless lines, I found myself leaning up against a large beam that was holding up one of the older World War II buildings.

As I stood in one of those long lines, I leaned against a beam in the building, my gaze drifting to a name etched partway up the wood. The carving, though painted over, was still legible. As I read it, a chill rippled through me, sending goosebumps from the top of my head down the back of my neck. The name read: *Victor E. Vasquez.* For a moment, I froze, my mind racing. *I remember thinking, could it really be my father's name? How many men in the Army could share not just his first name and last name but even the same middle initial?"*

I nearly dropped to my knees under the weight of the realization. How could it be that I was walking the same path my father once walked? A wave of sadness began to swell in my chest as I started to understand the depth of his silence and the quiet sincerity with which he had carried his burdens throughout his life.

It was weeks before I could call my dad and ask him if he remembered ever carving his name on a beam at Fort Lewis. He responded by saying yes, he carved his full name at every place he was stationed, including Fort Lewis. Since that time, I have always felt pride in knowing that I stood where my father, uncles, and cousins had stood before. I am not a warrior, nor have I ever wanted to be a warrior; all I ever wanted to do was give back and serve those who served me. I know now what it means to be a patriot. God bless all those young men and women and families that have given so much. My father was the only one in my family who served in the Pacific and was deployed for five years without ever coming home until the end. My dad served in the Army and received a Purple Heart, a Bronze Star, and seven battle stars while stationed on islands of the Pacific such as Corridor, Okinawa, Saipan, Iowa Jima, and in Manila of the Philippines.

***

Although my father was a quiet, almost an introverted man, he found a powerful outlet for self-expression through his gift for music. After long days of laboring in the fields under the scorching sun, he would often turn to his trumpet, letting its notes reveal the depths of his inner world. With each sound, it was as if his soul spoke, confessing emotions that words could never capture.

As we worked in the fields, music blasted through the humid

air, reaching every worker like a ritual gathering to harvest what the Aztec gods produced. However, this would not be our harvest. There was a constant sound of rancheras, the original country music, mirroring the passion of the Mexican culture. The melodic sounds were an opiate to the throbbing pain that grew as the day moved toward sunset. The sounds allowed young workers to dream or fantasize about dancing with that special person. I was too young for that and instead focused on how my father played tunes on his trumpet.

That trumpet carried notes of joyous revelry and sometimes a deep, soulful pain, depending on the song and occasion. Some melodies and harmonies alluded trauma of being Hispanic in a country of Whites. When I was young, I didn't understand that some people in the Anglo communities, the Gringos or Bolios as we used to call them. They seemed to fear our presence as much as we disliked their cold-hearted natures. When we spoke in Spanish, they seemed to be afraid of our language because they could not understand what we were saying. The young men reacted with anger quietly hiding a fear that we would run away with their young White girlfriends, or steal their possessions, but mostly that we might become a greater presence. Little did they know that all we ever wanted was to marry a Mexican woman to continue the Raza. My dad once recalled that when I was about three and still eating from a highchair, I looked at him while he was feeding me, and I said that I was going to marry a Mexican woman. Carrying forward lineage and our special culture mattered to me, even as a child.

Of course, fear was not all the Anglos felt for us. Hatred became a part of the daily formula for living in America. There were many White people who would go out of their way to make sure that we knew that they hated us and especially the thinking that they were better than us. The hatred and fear that I believed the Anglos had toward my community revealed itself in unexpected ways.

On one of our trips north, we stopped at a community in

West Texas and decided to have lunch in a local restaurant, something we rarely did. As we walked in, I noticed that the restaurant was filled with Anglos. We were the only Mexicans. After waiting about twenty minutes waiting to be seated, we sat ourselves down at a table in the middle of the room. We scanned the menu and waited for someone to serve us. After over forty-five minutes, no one came to ask if we were ready to order. I remember the glaring stares as we sat waiting, and I could feel a negative energy that told me it was not safe.

We were there long enough to watch other families arrive, get served, and leave after their meal. Then, the unexpected happened. My father, who was always quiet and accepting, got up and spread his arm across the table and swept everything onto the floor as he asked us to get up and leave this place. I watched him look toward the counter with people waiting there for lunch and tell them to f**k themselves. Hearing my father use a swear word was something we were not used to. After we got back to the car, my father said, "I spent five years fighting for this country, and I cannot even go into a restaurant with my family for a nice meal."

It seemed as though we were less than human to them; we were no more than slaves tending to the fields that brought an economy to those small communities all over the West, Pacific Northwest, the Midwest, and the Northeast. It felt like we were expendable; we could be replaced at any time.

Hatred was not an easy thing to live with, and it became very difficult to ignore, especially as we were reminded of it every day by waitresses who wouldn't serve us in restaurants, gas station attendants who wouldn't pump our gas or clean our windshields, and those who chose to call us spics, greasers, or beaners to our backs. The ones with the strongest opinions were usually the ones who would whisper "spic" or "greaser" once we had already walked by, as if we wouldn't be able to recognize where it came from. The most hateful people were usually as poor as we were and, in some cases, had a much more difficult life than we did because they did not have the close family ties that we had and cherished so much.

***

While my father never talked about the time he spent in the military, his service brought with it an opportunity to settle down in one place, for him to take a permanent job that would change our lives forever. My father decided to take a job at the Umatilla Army Depot, allowing us to drop out of the traveling caravan and live away from our home in Texas.

Things did not change very much after the decision to stay in Oregon. The pursuit of my education in my early years still met with similar challenges as before, without the ability to make any long-lasting friendships and always having to prove my ability to every new teacher in every new classroom with new classmates (more about this in later chapter). Yet this was not unlike the journey that my ancestors had been on since the beginning of my people or least we were taught that by the ancient ones. We were their direct descendants and our plight in life had a purpose for the good of all our people.

There is little stability in family life for those families that must constantly travel for work regardless of how far they must travel to get that job. Just for the record, we traveled to all these various places not because we were on vacation or because we enjoyed sightseeing, but because we were hungry. And no, we were not doing this because we liked what we were doing. We traveled north to survive.

CHAPTER 6
Campfire Stories

El que busca encuentra.
(If you search, you will find.)
~ Dicho

The typical evenings in the labor camp were spent sitting around the campfire behind the cabins of the migrant camp after working in scorching heat from sunup to sundown. The typical cabin revealed the brightness of day through the gaps in the wooden planks that served as the walls and the silence of darkness as the light began to disappear from those planks that held the structure together.

The campfire flames grew casting shadows of those who arrived serving to announce the beginning of the camp gathering. Anyone with a story to tell or just something to talk about is welcome to share. I missed my older brother Gerardo who often stayed in Mexico with family. I wished he could have heard the campfire stories shared by our elders as the night grew darker and the flames grew brighter, dancing with yellow, orange, and red bouncing off each other with occasional sparks leaping into the sky.

As the fire grew larger, the flames began to sparkle and dance from one brown face to another, and the stories of our ancestors began to sneak their way into whispered conversation.

One story as it was told by many of the elders was about La Llorona, the crying lady, who is said to wander the countryside looking for her children who had been lost to the brutalities of revolution and ancient wars between villages and the conquest. It didn't matter how far we traveled from Mexico, La Llorona would find us and remind us that she was still searching for those children who had left the Indian race to become mestizos.

La Llorona is said to be the ghost of Malintzin, as the Indians originally referred to her. She later became known as La Malinche, the Betrayer. La Malinche was an Indian woman who became one of the confidantes of Cortez and an advisor on Indian matters. She was the first to open the doors to foreigners and gave birth to one of the first mixed-race Indian babies, a child of Cortez. La Malinche or La Llorona is searching for those Indians lost to the Spanish conquest and those who were never born because of the new race created by mixing with Spanish blood.

As Raza, we have within us that constant struggle between the Spanish and Indian blood. I must respect that I have Spanish blood, but I am proud of and honor my Indian blood and the ancient stories. Over time the Indian culture will recreate the lost culture and La Malinche can rest in peace.

Of course, some of the best stories came from the young men who had been drinking the night before and who told us of their sightings. One such story came from my uncle Francisco, (Pancho) who had come home around 3:30 in the morning, shaky and pale. As he told it, La Llorna chased him down the road at sixty-five miles per hour, leaving scratch marks on the side of his car. She was trying to catch Francisco to see if he was one of the lost children. Later, I looked at his car for those scratch marks, and sure enough, they were there. Now I think maybe Francisco fell asleep at the wheel and drove off the country road through a barbed wire fence. I am still not brave enough to reject the idea that La Llorona is out there looking for my ancestors.

The greatest storytellers were the older women. They had the power to captivate, especially Tia Carmen, who had many stories about life during the Revolution. She would recount how she and Tia Lupe and Tia Rico would sneak out late at night walking several miles to feed soldiers of the Revolution who were hiding in the caves of an old mining field. They were ten to thirteen years old at the time. Like me, they could not take time out to be children. Tia Carmen would recall the federal soldiers riding their horses through Piedras Negras patrolling, looking for those who were giving aid to the revolutionaries.

Tia Carmen's best stories were always those that depicted the struggle between those who risked everything to help others and the people who only looked for their own greed. One of her stories was of a young boy who was walking home along the railroad tracks late at night. To his surprise a glowing rooster that looked as if it was a flame appeared in front of him, prancing, jumping, and kicking up its claws trying to get the boy's attention and enticing him to take it home. As the boy's interests wavered, the rooster's glow grew brighter, and when he decided to leave it and walk away, the rooster turned into a ball of flame and began to chase him all the way home. When he reached the door and turned to look before slamming it shut, the rooster stopped at the doorstep. When the boy went into his home for safety, he learned that his uncle had died, and the family members were mourning.

Tia Carmen could hypnotize everyone at the campfire for hours at a time. Her role was not just as storyteller. She always had a message for those youngsters who were out of control, like young colts kicking their heels in the wind to express their invulnerability. There was always a message about what was going on in our everyday life. I would be wondering if what I had done earlier in the day would summon a ball of fire to appear in front of me and try to capture my soul. Tia Carmen would always give me a reason to be good.

As the evening grew late, the old men, women and children left the campfire for their beds, which provided them with a temporary peace until daylight when they would have to face the fields again. The younger men always stayed later with a few of the older men to share the stories of the latest battle or to share a few drinks. During these times, I learned that there were several types of men, several types of courage, and that wisdom and intelligence were respected by most of the traveling group.

At age nine, the campfire was a place for me to absorb lessons on life and how to be a good person, father, and warrior. I watched men who brought their families to the campfire and the attention they paid to their children or how, from time to time, they took whispered direction from their wives. Those families that were the closest came together and left together. They worked and played together and there was always laughter.

I saw, too, the young men who drank too much as they began boasting of conquests over other men they had defeated in battle. Of course, no one ever knew who they were or when they were defeated. Later as the drinks came more frequent and plentifully, it was the same men who also boasted of their romantic abilities and the young women who were interested in capturing them as a prize. At nine, I already knew that these were the men the young women of the camp laughed at when they walked across the camp trying to entice the same young women into their future.

There were hard lessons to be learned behind the flickering of the campfire light, such as how to survive when another young man challenges you with his fists. At every camp, there were a couple of families with a code of violence, and if they weren't fighting with someone else, they were fighting with each other. The campfire was where I experienced my first fight that drew blood, and it was the first time that my mind left my body, and I felt no pain. The men were drinking and bragging about their exploits in combat when they began to compare the attributes of one young man to another. I was one of those young men.

I became the center of discussion when one of my uncles

declared that I could beat any boy my size or age in boxing. There it was, out in the open, a challenge to the whole camp. I was the one who had to prove my worthiness, and I didn't even know why. Of course, one of the family members found a match for me, one of Los Changos. The fight was scheduled for the following evening after work. I had an entire workday to consider my fate. I didn't even know how to fight.

That fateful evening, I felt like vomiting. I didn't know what to expect. I was shaken by the fear of not knowing what to do and there was no one to guide me. Once my uncle committed me to the fight, none of my family members intervened, and this is one of the few times my father was working at a different farm and not around so I could not seek advice or protection. I was responsible for showing up at the appointed time behind the cabins next to the strawberry field that had been picked clean that day. As I waited for my adversary, I noticed the red splatters of strawberry juice against the dark ground and remember wondering if my blood would look like that against my dark skin. I could see empty strawberry flats smeared with the same bright red from the delicious fruit we had picked all that day. Just as I began to focus on the beauty of the field and hear the birds off in the distance, the men began to show up.

The men were emptying the little cabins after checking in with their families. They were ready for the entertainment. As I stood there awaiting my fate, something shifted. It was as if the event had nothing to do with me. I was hoping that it was all a mistake and that I would be a spectator.

Spellbound Around Campfires

Hot blue and orange flames burning

The souls of their shoes exposed.

Shadows dancing with the flames

Bouncing up and down like an outdoor ballet.

Sweet smells of leather, locust trees burning

Slipping into tar-papered shacks with studded walls.

Echoes of young men opening another beer,

Hey loco, get me another Oly.

Sounds of cars passing in the distance

A highway not traveled by a migrant.

Leading to homes with open-beamed ceilings, skylights,

Wall-to-wall carpeting and a Jacuzzi.

The ad reads, $0 down, owner will pay closing,

FHA/VA approved, why pay rent, Migrant!

The fire burns as an old man speaks.

In a forgotten language,

Indians put down their beers.

An old man with an old prophecy

Of Indians reclaiming old lands of corn

A thousand centuries of highways north and south

Your home is covered by the Aztec Sun

Surrounded by the walls of Atzlan.

Finally, I knew the time was near. Tio Pancho was approaching with the man they called Willie La Rana (Willie the Toad). I always found it curious how he came to get that name, for he didn't look like a toad. In our culture, there was an interesting custom of identifying people by names other than their given ones. These nicknames were often inspired by animals, plants, or objects that bore some resemblance to a person's appearance or behavior. For instance, members of my family were affectionately referred to as "los camotes."

The story behind this nickname goes back to my great uncles, who were twins born at home. When the first twin was brought out to be introduced to the family, someone remarked, "Mira, se mira como un camote"— "Look, he looks like a sweet potato." From that moment on, the name stuck and became a part of our family's identity.

As my uncle and Willie La Rana approached, my heart began to pound loud enough for the men to hear my fear. At least, I thought everyone could hear it. After all, this would be my first fight. It was already too late for training or last-minute instruction. All I could hope for was that my tio or even one of my tias, like Tia Carmen, would notice and stop what was about to happen.

No such luck. It was the way of things and a time for me to begin to learn to survive. As my uncle and Willie La Rana got closer, I could see my opponent. I didn't even know his first name, to me he was one of the Changos a nickname given to family of boys from my hometown. I began to realize there was no backing out. I was about to have a fight with someone I knew as one of the Changos and there was no reason I could think of that we should fight at all.

Silence fell over the field, and a small circle began to form around me and the other young boy, whose first name I never knew and the two fight promoters, Pancho, and Willie La Rana. As the circle closed, I knew there was no escape. My manhood and family name were at stake, and it was my time to become a warrior. I didn't want anyone to think that one of the Vasquez boys would run to his cabin for safety. I would hold my ground no matter what came my way.

My uncle grabbed me by the arm and brought me to the center of the gladiator's circle. As I looked up, I noticed the other boy being given some pre-fight instructions just like the professionals on the Friday night fights. Now we faced each other for the first time, I could see his light brown eyes staring at me. It seemed that he was wondering why I was there to fight him. There was no way to tell what he was thinking, but I knew that he could see the fear in my eyes, or at least it felt like he and all the other men in the camp could tell that I was afraid.

God, I felt like running away! That was not possible, however. It would never be possible for the rest of my life. Once I walked behind those broken-down cabins and into the strawberry field arena, it was too late to look back. This moment had been decided whether I walked away from fear or not. I chose to stay.

Pancho set the stage for the fight. He began by asking us to face each other. My heart began to pound even harder, and I found it more difficult to breathe. It became so difficult that I had to open my mouth to catch my breath. It felt as if it would be the end of my life. There was no way that I would survive this.

My uncle yelled out, "Start fighting." We both stood there staring at each other, not knowing what to do, when suddenly, I felt someone grab the back of my neck and push my face up against the other boy's face.

Our faces collided, and my lip began to bleed and swell. I began to hear a ringing sound, and I lost track of the people who had been there before. At the same time, instantly, I knew what to do. I began punching the boy's face like a well-trained boxer in a championship fight. With every ounce of strength, I calculated each punch with the precision of a watchmaker. In fact, I could visualize my next punch. As I threw my punches one after another, I saw him start to go down. I began kicking his chest like I would a football for an extra point. He started to get up, but my punching and kicking continued until he went down again. I kept punching, and as he stayed down again, I kept kicking.

The fight seemed like an eternity, although now I know it only lasted a few minutes. Covered with blood from his nose to his chin, he looked at me and smiled. I will never forget the strength I saw in my opponent's eyes. He never quit. He kept trying to get up to fight until he had no energy left, and he refused to cry out. This was the first time I felt the power of guilt. I felt guilty about the violence that I allowed to take over my mind and body and the fact that I had caused harm to another human being.

This was when I learned that I had a person inside of me who would do anything to survive and that I didn't like that person very much, even if those instincts would save my life later. I would always be overwhelmed with guilt about the violence that could erupt from me with little prompting. This would not be the last time that I would have to experience those feelings, feelings that would allow me to cause pain to someone who could have been my friend. Those feelings would, however, protect me and help me survive in dangerous situations. I found that I could detach myself from my kinder side, the side that took care of my little sister and cooked meals for my brother and sisters, and become a person totally focused on surviving. I later understood this person and learned to control that burst of focused negative energy.

That night in the strawberry field, I learned about my other side. This was not how I lived every day, but it was a negative energy that could be unleashed when needed. I learned this energy was a force that needed to be respected and controlled. I learned I could control pain by escaping with my mind and had the gift of being able to control my environment with my mind.

The fight was finally over, and I stood victorious without cheers of joy in empty triumph. My mind was full of questions about what had just happened. What sense could there be in fighting someone I didn't really know. Sometimes, young children are much wiser than the adults who are trying to raise them. To this day I know that young boy and I should have been friends. I learned over time that the men who were there to watch the fight had lived a life of violence, having learned at an early age that you needed to defend yourself when going to the northern land where in an instant you could fall victim to those who rejected our music, language, culture, and color. My uncle put me in the ring to teach me how to fight and defend myself. It turns out that he had been jumped by three White men in Chicago and the only thing that saved him was his ability to fight.

Living in the labor camps didn't produce many lifelong friends because the crops controlled our lives, and each camp only lasted a few weeks. My aunts, uncles, and cousins became my best friends because they were always there, traveling with us from camp to camp. We lived from week to week and from crop to crop. As the fields began to look more manicured with the weeding completed and the plants beginning to mature, I knew that it would soon be time to move on.

We worked our way from California to Oregon, then on to Washington where we spent most of our summer traveling to many little towns in the Yakima Valley, towns like Mabton, Toppenish, and Grandview. They were always different but also always the same. In most of these towns, we could expect to drive down the main street and find a Rexall drugstore with its orange lettering and that funny X in the design. Going into town was not a daily activity. We usually went on Sundays, the day when we took a break from our hoes, the hot sun, and the potato and egg tacos we had for lunch. In most cases, we picked up supplies such as hair spray, razor blades, shaving cream, and occasionally nylon stockings for my aunts.

There was always a theater in the middle of town, and sometimes that provided us with some entertainment. But those times were rare since I did not speak a word of English. Occasionally, we found a theater with movies from Mexico. One of my favorite actors was Cantinflas, a famous comedian who could make anyone in the world laugh. Cantinflas could endear himself to entire communities by stumbling and falling all over himself, but he would always get the last laugh. We could usually find a Mexican restaurant with food like we could get at home, and often, the owners came from South Texas or northern Mexico. When we did go to a restaurant, it was usually on Sunday afternoons right after the eleven o'clock mass where the men would atone for the sins they had committed at the dance the night before.

Saturdays were always workdays unless a hard rain came by the grace of God to grant us an extra day of rest. Usually, we were out in the fields early, as always, but on Saturdays, we could expect the dance that evening, usually held in a warehouse or abandoned building where Mexicans could gather in large numbers. The dances were normally held in places outside of the city limits. I never gave it a second thought until later in life, that most of our social activities were held away from the main part of the community, except for Sunday afternoon picnics, probably because the parks were usually in the center of town.

Saturday evenings were time to get ready for the dance. The young men rushed to the camp from the fields, raising dust with their speeding cars as they raced to the cabins to be first in line for the shower. Most of the showers were the same in each camp: a long room with four to six showerheads and wooden pallets on the floor for us to walk on so we wouldn't have to step on the bare cement or dirt floors.

Some of the rednecks would say to us, "You clean up nice." What they were trying to say is that we were less threatened when we were out of our work clothes.

The young men brought out their finest dress clothes: fancy

custom-made Western boots handmade by craftsman in Mexico and a colorful Western-style shirt, sometimes topped with a bolo tie and Stetson hat. All the fancy dress clothes were to increase the possibility of attracting the most eligible young ladies. The young ladies were so fine with their colorful dresses of purple, red, and turquoise colors used by our ancient ancestors in depicting historical events on the pyramids. As the dance hall began to fill up, families were everywhere, with little children running from one end of the hall to the other.

The little boys wore dark pants and white shirts, usually a bolo tie and cowboy boots. After all, we were the first vaqueros in North America. The little girls commonly wore white or pink chiffon with lace and black patent leather shoes. It was mostly a family event whenever any celebration occurred, and Saturday nights were a celebration. With the dance hall overflowing, the kegs of beer began to screech out that familiar sound of gases escaping from the king's tomb. This announced that it was time for the beer to be served, and the men lined up for a glass. This included me, young as I was it was all right for me to drink with the grown men if a family member was with me.

Oh! Then, that wonderful music started, and the mood of the dance hall changed. Everyone began to move their feet and exchanged glances with anyone who looked back.

Ay, que lindas! Oh, how lovely those Indian women from an ancient land in the new world looked and how they could dance! As a boy, I was hypnotized by the swaying of their hips from side to side and in a circular motion, bringing me an innocent pleasure and satisfaction in just watching. I had not yet received the curse of adulthood with the need to touch the forbidden flesh of the girls, much less pursue love in the back seat of a 1956 Ford.

My pleasure was watching everyone and dancing occasionally with my cousin Esperanza, whom we called Bebe. We were good friends. Our closeness came from knowing that something in our lives was wrong but not knowing what it was. We understood each other's questions.

As the early evening greeted the late evening and the beer took its effect, we began to hear periodic yells of "Viva Mexico!"

Dancing was not always enough for people to forget their daily struggles and the fight for life that occurred every day. Some of the young men took their anger and frustration out on other men in the camp. It was always easier to strike out at the closest person to you, especially after a night of drinking, dancing, and having to think about going home without the young Indian girl who eluded everyone at the dance to protect herself from the wrath of her parents. How the young women broke hearts! We heard of the conquests and the defeats throughout the following week as we walked through the fields with our hoes in hand and our dreams of what was possible just beyond the next field.

The tragedy of these wonderful dances, these diversions from the everyday struggles, is that from time to time, someone would lose control and start a fight. The worst was when the fight led to deadly force like the time El Gordo, Julian the Fat One, pulled a knife on a young man from the neighboring camp and cut him across the gut. All I could see was a gush of blood and a white shirt turning the color of strawberry juice. He grabbed at his stomach as if he were holding his guts in place so they wouldn't fall out and scatter on the floor.

This was the first time I saw fear in another person's eyes. It was also the first time I realized with a shock that death could be a moment away and that I had no control over the guaranteed protection of my life. It was the first time I witnessed a knife fight that led to serious wounds that could have killed someone, but it would not be the last. I have had to stare at a shotgun in my face and dodge bullets trying to enter a bar that I should not have been in in the first place. Growing up would be hard, with some tough lessons on survival and an early education in human nature. The greatest weapon for survival was listening and paying attention to all the communication, verbal and nonverbal, watching all the activities at the same time, knowing when to move, and most important of all, knowing where all the exits were.

As a young boy, I developed and internalized an early philosophy I didn't realize until later in life. The knifing behind the dance hall was not the last time I would see the blood of my jente, my people, spilled by another from the community. It was difficult enough facing hatred from the Anglo Americans without our own people fighting each other.

An early lesson was not to fear what I didn't and couldn't control. This attitude allowed me to accept a special kind of fear, the kind that gave me blind courage to face danger with resignation but with respect that fate would hand me the right set of instructions. I became a risk-taker because after all, my fate had already been decided, that somewhere unknown to me would be my place and time.

Fate alone would not guide my life, and my treatment of others became a more critical piece of my daily living. As I began to see the results of my actions and what they brought me, I noticed that if I allowed my dark side to rule my behavior, adverse events would follow. However, if I treated others with kindness and thought of the consequences of my actions, life would be more tolerable. I guess it holds with the old saying that what goes around comes around. The rule was remarkably simple: Don't do anything to anyone that you wouldn't want to be done to you.

CHAPTER 7
Aztlán and The Seven Caves

Today we are at last beginning to understand the intricacies of this amazing culture, which was the equal of any in Europe in moral refinement, artistic sensibility, social complexity, and political organization.

~ J. Jorge Klor de Alva
(Foreword to *The Broken Spears*)

Now that you know some of my childhood background, I'd like to share a large cornerstone of my ancestral belief system. This has everything to do with a special story—Aztlán and The Seven Caves.

Not every child is fortunate enough to have first-hand immersion in ancient cultures, especially their very own ancestral backstories. How fortunate that I learned about my Nahua lineage as a child—the Indigenous people of Mexico, El Salvador, Guatemala, Honduras, and Nicaragua. My ancestors in the south-central region of Mexico were the Aztecs, who had knowledge of Aztlán and the Seven Caves.

The story of Aztlán and the Seven Caves is foundational to who I am, where I'm from, and where I'm going. The story was shared in oral tradition from generation to generation and is one of the greatest gifts my relatives passed down to me. It opened me to past-present-future philosophical insights as nothing else could. An overview of this ancient legend will help readers understand a culture so quite different to their own. The beliefs and practices of my ancestors touched minds, bodies, and souls in ways that most U.S. citizens cannot discern without a primer.

Aztlán and the Seven Caves introduce the mystical lore and legend of the origins of my people as well as the positive outcomes of native beliefs and the concept of a great quest. I am hopeful that these reflections will serve today's young people struggling with the unpredictability of the future and of living in a foreign world that does not greet them with arms outstretched. May it bolster their spirits and resiliency if they get too close and are pushed away.

I am now an American (U.S. citizen), but my bloodline originated from the Mesoamericans (1300s), and perhaps prior to the pre-Columbian Mexican civilization between 1800 and 300 BC.

Sitting in my home in Alexandria, Virginia, I feel the guilt of not returning to my ancient lands, especially now that I have gifts and knowledge to give back. My education, daily life struggles, intellect developed through the errors of my choices, and counsel from my role models—all of this should be returned to the people who ushered me toward my present-day existence.

***

As you read this chapter, keep in mind the themes of questing, migrating, wandering, and searching. These themes reflect my experiences as a migrant worker and encapsulate the Aztecs. Today's immigrants are following the spirits of their ancestors, traveling to unfamiliar lands in pursuit of a predestined place, a place of truth. There, they are meant to find, settle, populate, and fulfill their destiny.

As John Collier (author of *The Indians of the Americas*) states:

> *The Aztecs' life was one of efficient, many-sided*

> *agriculture; of craftsmanship unexcelled in the Western Hemisphere or the world; of much democracy in human relationships. Its social base was the exogamous clan, and within the clan, leadership was achieved and kept through proved individual merit. Clans united into tribes, with equal representation on the tribal council; and the council chose the tribal functionaries based on demonstrated merit. There existed rank, but not caste, the only exception being the quite fluid, shifting slave class. The slave controlled his own family and could in turn hold slaves; none were born into slavery; murder of a slave brought the death penalty to the killer; slavery became a temporary status while a man expiated a crime; often families of the poor would rotate their children, one at a time, into temporary slavery…*

Likewise, books might focus on these sacrifices from a Westernized viewpoint or from the perspective of the conquerors—the Christian Spaniards—without opposing context. After all, history is written by the victors. This misses the truth of the Aztecs' true focus, which was foreknowledge of their impending doom, the mandate to quest, and the promise of finding "home." Thus, the lore shared with me by my family may differ from what you read online or in historical journals. However, what was passed down verbally has survived centuries and is as authentic in my view as any other account.

Because of my ancestors, I can write with the freedom of a brilliantly colored parrot flying through the Yucatan. I've developed a passion for painting the jungle with words, like a poet. My life in the U.S. has given me the strength of a monarch butterfly that returns to Mexico every year to make sure that the life cycle continues. It is an honor to share my faraway musings about the Aztlán and the Seven Caves and their impact on me today.

It is common knowledge that each cave was dedicated to a Nahau group—Xochimilca, Tlahuica, Acolhua, Tlaxcalteca, Tepaneca, Chalca, and Mexica. This is documented in history books. But what isn't common knowledge is that my very own Mexican ancestors would eventually leave their newfound homes to seek the place of origin, Aztlán and the Seven Caves on a quest to find a sense of belonging after centuries of searching.

It is crucial to understand the deeper context behind the fall of the Aztec Empire—a time steeped in prophecy and misinterpretation. To truly grasp why Emperor Motecuhzoma welcomed Hernán Cortés, one must consider the profound significance of a long-held prophecy that foretold the arrival of foreign invaders. According to Aztec belief, Quetzalcoatl, a revered deity, revealed that one invader from the east would bring change and perhaps destruction.

When Cortés and his men landed on the shores of the Aztec Empire in the early 16th century, Motecuhzoma did not simply see a Spaniard with imperial ambitions. To him, and to many of his people, the pale-skinned, bearded Cortés bore an uncanny resemblance to the descriptions of the invaders as foretold in their prophecy. This perception shaped Motecuhzoma's decisions ultimately sealed the fate of his empire.

Modern references, like the phrase "Motecuhzoma's revenge," often trivialize this catastrophic period of history without acknowledging its complex roots. The fall of the Aztec Empire was not merely the result of military conquest but a collision of belief, destiny, disease and deception.

According to Irwin R. Blacker's *Cortés and the Aztec Conquest* (available on Amazon): *"In their quest for gold, and for the ruler who controlled its steady flow into the Aztec treasuries, the conquistadors had indeed marched far—some 275 miles over mountainous country to the great Valley of Mexico."* The author adds (regarding Cortés): *"Even after his god-like reputation had been shattered, and his horses and cannons were no longer regarded as supernatural, his ruthless daring took him on to victory. Yet in the end, his prize was not the gold that he had sought, but the destruction of the entire Aztec civilization."*

Interestingly, much of the word-of-mouth legend and lore I was taught as a child are corroborated through these quotes and in the book *The Broken Spears: The Aztec Account of the Conquest of Mexico* by Miguel Leon-Portilla (available on Amazon). Imagine my surprise and delight when my memories of childhood campfire stories aligned with these authors, especially the renowned Mexican historian, translator, and author Miguel Leon-Portilla. I shape many of my recollections from insights in his book to give readers context about the broken spears and what it means to the ancestors of the Aztecs today.

In a nutshell, seven bad omens indicated the end of the Aztec world, including lights in the sky and supernatural creatures, in the late 1400s. Then another bad omen appeared in the sky ten years prior to the invasion of the Spaniards in the early 1500s.

There were betrayals. In a "If you can't beat them, join them" tactic, the Tlaxcala joined the Cortés forces against Motecuhzoma. The traitors helped massacre the unarmed Cholultecas nearby, fulfilling the prophetic plundering of Tenochtitlán, which was ongoing. Two parties were deployed to stop Cortés in the Valley of Mexico but failed. By now, Motecuhzoma feared for his people but left the outcome to fate without defensive action, even though his brother, Cuitláhuac, reminded him of the massacre of the Cholultecas. Again, Motecuhzoma believed what was foretold and that the Spaniards would ultimately claim the right to rule.

Cortés traveled toward Tenochtitlán from the south and arrived at Xoloco, near the gated entrance to the city. Motecuhzoma greeted Cortés with gifts and was told he had nothing to fear. However, when Cortés was inside the royal palace, he took Motecuhzoma captive and raided the treasury of gold. Motecuhzoma's soldiers were massacred, and the city was blockaded. People starved, had no fresh water, and were exposed to disease but continued to fight for their lives. It was a losing battle.

Motecuhzoma's brother, Cuitláhuac, was now on the throne and surrendered to Cortés, begging for death. Thus, the Aztec empire fell to the Spaniards. And today, when travelers to Mexico speak of "Motecuhzoma's revenge," I must wonder if Motecuhzoma confuses hapless visitors with invaders and pours out his wrath. Could you blame him?

Aztlán Through the Eyes of a Boy

Now that a historical snapshot makes this saga clearer, we can take a closer look at Aztlán and the Seven Coves from a boyhood perspective of curiosity. Aztlán was steeped in mysteries understood only by the spiritual tribal leaders. This historical journey began as a vision of a place they spoke of a place ten generations into the future, a place that called out to its people to seek and find. Even today, we searched for hidden knowledge. We search to discover our individual missions and our place in the world.

The precursor was that many ancient generations had lived in comfort, which led to lives without purpose. Our people began to question their existence. *Why are we here, and what should we be doing? What should we be seeking?* they wondered. The unsettling feelings captured our spirit and eventually led us to leave Aztlan and begin our migration, wandering in search of a greater truth, one that would help us realize the harmony between human beings and the earth and what would be needed to sustain our needs. We migrated southward with no knowledge of time or place other than trusting that a sign would point to the place of settlement, a sign known only to the high priest, who was guided by spiritual writings.

My people left as a tribe on a massive exodus to search for the mythical place from which our people would arise to assume their role on this earth. It was foretold by the priests that the place we would search for would reveal itself to the spiritual elders. We would embark on a journey with little knowledge of where this new place would be. We were destined to wander from the birthplace of the Aztec people to what the ancestors believed would be our chosen destination, a place that had been gifted to them to explore the secrets of the mother, the earth we lived on and walked on.

The Aztec people's journey had been prophesied by a high priest, who, from a scroll, revealed instructions on when to begin the journey form our place of origin. The instruction was to find a sacred place that was described as an island covered with the purity of truth, an island surrounded by water and the plumage of a white heron. This mythical place would hold the key to the beginning of life for the Aztec people and those who had come before them.

In the sacred stories repeated generation after generation, we were described as rising from the heron's feathers and living in a magical place with abundant wildlife and vegetation after we emerged from seven caves in the bowels of the earth in a place called Aztlán. The most recent migration of our people occurred after the Conquista (conquest and invasion) of the Spaniards, a period that brought separation as our families, bodies, and souls were torn apart by violence against our will. The Conquista had been prophesied in ancient writings but in little detail. The writings could not have predicted the greed of the men that came, the destruction they would bring to our families, and our religious beliefs.

Thus, the second part of the myth of Aztlán began with the Aztec's arrival in the northwestern part of what is Mexico today and eventually to the valley of Mexico City in the central plateau. The place to settle was a valley chosen by the priests. The valley was already home to existing tribes that had arrived from civilizations to the south. Each tribe claimed its tribal territory within the boundaries of a large and fertile valley with a vast lake that sat in the center of a vast and bountiful valley. Tribes, from time to time, invaded each other's territory, sometimes taking captives and often melding cultures and families, creating an emerging new culture that combined from the northern part of the world with the south. The Aztecs became dominant and the most powerful, most influential, and most resented of all the tribes.

The centuries that passed brought with them wars against foreigners with white skin and red hair, wars against the aliens' way of life, and conflicts with cultures, forcing us to give way to food, medicines, and those life-giving practices that had once belonged to only one people. What we gained from such invasions was assimilation and the creation of the mestizo (people of mixed Indian and European blood). This blending of race and cultures allowed us to gain greater knowledge in preparation for the rebirth of Aztlán. Could the same hold true today? Does the racial intermingling and blending of DNA, over time, create a truer form for all of us? Certainly, not everyone approves of mixing DNA. Many believe the greatest respect is retaining a pure lineage, the purest succession possible.

Some in my own family caution against this blending of bloodlines, as you'll see. They do so with the best of intentions, not out of prejudice but out of a sense of preservation. I ponder a bigger picture, however—a race comprised of humanity rather than pockets of skin color, clan, or nationality. If we are all human, aren't we all one? What if the Aztecs, through their wanderings on Earth, managed to disseminate a portion of themselves into humankind's biology? What if we now document the unique journeys and the histories of our past to forge a peaceful path toward oneness? Is that too much wishful thinking? Is that what the Aztecs foresaw?

I sense that my own difficult path spans more than those ten generations spoken by the Aztecs and, indeed, bridges the past while linking to the future. It merges two worlds: the ancient world embroidered with threads of ancestral Indian ways and the threads of the future that have been blended into daily lives, even today, through myth and prophecy. Our present world offers confusion and begs for a place to turn to for the answers.

Only then can the questions of who we are and where we are bound to be revealed.

We now live in a time that has caused us to humble ourselves, waiting for the gods to show us the sign. We have lost many of the families that were the original travelers to the temptations of another world of Whiteness.

The temptations that often begin as innocent acts of survival are captured in the ancient *dicho* (Mexican proverb), *Una Mosca en la Leche* (A Fly in the Milk.) This saying warns of the danger the fly faces when drawn to the sweet nourishment of the milk. At first, it hovers on the rim, drawn by its tempting scent. But as desire grows, the fly ventures closer, risking too much for a taste of what it believes will sustain it. Consumed by its hunger, the fly dives too deep and drowns, undone by the very thing that enticed it.

This metaphor serves as a cautionary tale for navigating identity in a world rich with cultures and experiences. The risk lies in immersing ourselves so deeply in understanding another culture or race that we lose sight of our own roots. Without grounding, we may become adrift, unable to reconcile who we are with where we came from. To thrive, we must embrace the duality of learning from others while staying firmly rooted in our heritage. Knowing who we are and where we come from is essential to understanding where we are going.

The original path was embedded in my mind, but there was always the risk of choosing the wrong path because of weakness and the evolving temptations of the new world.

CHAPTER 8
Leemel

In Náhuatl, the language of the Aztec world, one key word for poet was "tlamatine," meaning "the one who knows," or "he who knows something." Poets were considered "sages of the word," who meditated on human enigmas and explored the beyond, the realm of the gods.

~ Edward Hirsch, American poet, and critic.

A fleeting overview of Aztlán and the Seven Caves is one thing. A deeper dive is quite another. I'm so very, very fortunate that my childhood was spent absorbing lore and legends while traveling from place to place. The storytelling was better than anything I could have heard on the radio or seen on television. As I've mentioned, those early years of migrant farm work were filled with entertainment in the form of ancient history lessons that instilled a sense of pride and wonder in my young heart.

Listening as the narratives unfolded, I began to understand how my people came to be wired as artists, students of natural medicines, healers, priests, warriors, and writers. I began to understand why my people were—and are—wanderers. We always had been so since the Aztecs went on their quest after a violent and destructive invasion by the Spaniards.

The Lore of Leemel

One story touched a chord in my heart because it involved a

child like me, a curious and imaginative boy. Most stories are about grown people of glorious status—rulers and conquerors. But this story was about another sort of hero, the boy named Leemel. It's a legacy story with a fuller view of why the Aztlán and the Seven Caves legend was passed down for generations in the first place. It's a story about why we wander, migrate, and are who we are.

It will take you, dear reader, into a raw and revealing antiquity tale with a clearer understanding, and I hope it resonates with you as it has with me. Through my father and uncles, I learned of Leemel, who existed in the distant past. He, like me, learned at the knee of village elders and absorbed lessons of antiquity and the lore of our people. And this is what I was told and later transcribed for posterity to the best of my ability. Here goes.

***

A boy, Leemel, sat around the communal fire, listening to ancient reminiscences passed down and foreseeing the future, he noticed that the village elders always disagreed and debated with one another. Their conversations conjured images of the ancient homeland. He could visualize what it might have looked like and how it might have been to live in a place that provided for every basic human need. How could there be any place that provided whatever you might need?

What escaped his commonsense thoughts was an understanding of why the leaders of the ancient tribe would have chosen to leave Aztlán in the first place. Why would anyone decide to abandon a place of comfort and choose a life of wandering, never knowing if there would be enough food to support the tribe? *Why would we agree to leave a place that was always spoken of as bountiful, where everyone had what they needed?* he thought.

While the high priest spoke to the leaders, Leemel stood silent, trying to visualize this mythical place always described as covered with a blanket of white, bountiful with waterfowl, fish, and brilliantly colored birds with bodies of black and heads of red. He wondered whether he could find this place. Was it possible to return to the place his people had chosen to leave? Even if he wanted to return, he would not know how to get there. Would it still be the same? What would remain after so many centuries of wandering in search of a truth that had eluded even the priest who had spoken of it for so many years?

When the debate seemed to pause, Leemel struggled to build up his courage and interrupt the conversation. "What is this land that we talk about, a place that lacks for nothing, covered with a blanket of white over the land surrounded by mountains, a place that we call Aztlán?"

Three elders turned slowly to Leemel, curiously looking at him. They could not believe this young man would probe beyond the limits of acceptable courtesies, limits that had been established and respected for centuries. Why did this boy want to know as much as the priests?

As the elders sat in silence, pondering their response, Leemel nervously wondered what the outcome of his bold question would be. As the elders whispered among themselves, the oldest of the three agreed to be the spokesperson. His face bore witness to his exposure to the sun, with trails of travel in the wrinkles covering his face, placed there like an explorer's map that marked his numerous journeys. The old priest turned to Leemel and said, "I will talk with you of the great journey that continues."

The elder, whose name Leemel did not know, walked toward him, and sat with him near the fire. The priest turned his body slowly, revealing a twisted leg. By his side was a cane made of a wood that Leemel knew could not be found in his valley. The priest began by saying, "I will first describe for you the location of the place of Whiteness." He described the landmarks that pointed to a great valley surrounded by towering mountains that looked like teeth biting the sky. "In the middle of the towering mountains is a valley. This valley is the place of the seven caves."

The old man began to smile. "Aztlán is a place of the spirit."

Leemel looked at the old man with bewilderment. "Is Aztlán a place where the ancient spirits live?"

"No," the old man said. "It is a place of the spirit, a place that lives in your soul, a place that is inside you and everyone who is a descendant of the original people. Aztlán belongs to the original peoples who care for and caress the breast of this great earth by planting, watering, and harvesting crops to produce only what we need—the food we eat. They are the people who sweat over the earth with their heart in the soul of the seven caves, only to provide what the house and land of Aztlán call for. It is a place that guides your morality as it has guided our ancestors who rose from the earth through the seven caves to the place of Whiteness. From the seven caves, there came to be seven tribes that lived in harmony for many centuries, sharing hunting grounds and cultivating the water gardens next to each other in their canoes. It was a land that provided abundance for our people, a land that required little in return."

The elder paused and continued. "Our relatives of the ancient times lived in this place for many generations before they began the long journey. Not many people in this new land know the location of our place of beginning."

Leemel thought back and said, "I once overheard my great-grandfather describe the place of our origin and how to get there. His father gave him the information but could not recall all the details."

"Yes," the elder said, "it was passed from father to son. I am passing on the location to you because I have no family. They all left this world, sick from the illness of the new people."

Leemel nodded. He didn't know what else to say.

"Aztlán is located north of this valley, and it takes many months of traveling to get to the northernmost point. A point where the mountains with teeth reflect in a lake just south of the valley that constantly boils with the gods' anger and shoots out its lifeblood twenty-four times in one day. To the east, the boundary of Aztlán does not go beyond the land of red earth and great sunsets. To the west, if you follow the river that flows like a snake on the hunt to the great river that flows into the lake without an end, where the sun goes to rest, you will come to that northernmost boundary of Aztlán. In the other direction, where the green of the earth meets the brown earth and where hidden serpents live is the southernmost boundary. The outer boundary of the valley of Aztlán is where the brown earth covered with sand and lacking the water to nourish the plants to feed the tribes begins. That was the beginning point for our people. The journey began somewhere in the center of this land where you will find an island surrounded by water with a mountain in the center spiraling toward the sky and reaching for the Sun God."

The old man sighed. "And remember," he reminded Leemel, "Aztlán is a place of the spirit, a place that you carry with you if you are one of us. Being part of the tribe, belonging to us, is determined by the way you live your life. Our people lived with a sense of satisfaction, with plenty of food, water, and plants for sustenance. They fished the great fish from the lake surrounding the city and cultivated the bounty from water gardens that produced corn, tomatoes, and chilies for all to eat. Our land produced enough so that we had an abundance of seeds, enough for the birds and for trading with other villages. Our people lived together in harmony with the land and the wildlife for many generations without turmoil. Peace and harmony were a part of Aztlán since the beginning of time since we walked out of the seven caves."

The elder sighed again and was quiet for a long moment. Then he spoke. "It was the priests who brought questions into the lives of the villagers, from the new knowledge of the prophecy that had been brought to the priests by the god Huitzilopochtli. A need to search for the truth began to grow from the new teachings. The high priest began to seek answers as to why some of our people would be asked to leave Aztlán to search for a new place that would provide continued sustenance. But the truth has escaped our tribes since we began our journey.

Leemel asked, "If we are here, far away from the ancient land, does that mean that every soul of the land left this beautiful world to wander in search of the truth and left our city unprotected, abandoned for eternity?"

"No!" the elder said. "Not everyone left the ancient land. Some remained to continue the lifecycle that had begun there, but many had to leave so as not to empty the soul of our earth."

The elder rested in silence a few more moments, then added, "It was decided that to preserve the spirit of the seven caves, many of our people would have to leave the comfort of our world. They were asked to go out onto the earth to find the greater truth of living in harmony with her. Eventually, we would return with the knowledge that could be used by all the people of Atzlan. The people needed to leave the land they loved so much for the earth to continue living as we knew it. Without the journey, the ancient land would have died from the exhaustion of providing for all its children."

"Now that we are here in this valley of lakes surrounded by mountains, is this all of the people who began the journey?" Leemel asked.

The elder's face turned sad. "No. Some continued the journey going further south, where the land is full of trees so dense only the strongest of plants can grow, where there are little animals with the faces of humans living in the giant trees. Places where there are many birds, the colors of a rainbow, and many fruits that grow wild. We have met travelers from that region who have come to visit from time to time, and as we talked, we have come to know that they are of us by the stories they carry in their spirit. They came from Aztlán. Our people have wandered the earth as we know it."

Leemel noticed that as the elder recounted the ancient stories passed down from generation to generation, his eyes watered with sorrow at being so distant from the land that gave life to the Aztec people, the people from Aztlán.

The elder lifted his head and said to Leemel, "We are at another point in our earth's history, one that is calling for our people to take another journey. As a people, we are at a crossroads. The priests have been told by the gods that the life-giving earth is not pleased with us and that we must not challenge her when she demands respect. We have challenged the patience of her ability to produce from her breasts the nourishment to give life to everyone in the village."

How could we abandon such a great city? wondered Leemel.

Since they arrived in this new place, the ancient tribe has been known to build towers for observing the stars, great temples for worshipping, and halls for the great warriors who defended the city from invaders. The builders of the city used the ancient knowledge passed on through families but always held in safe keeping by the high priest on scrolls of sheepskin. The knowledge of the culture was held by the high priest to be passed on when there were no heirs to the inheritance. The ones who became writers, astronomers, mathematicians, doctors, and artists were born into their profession.

Many of the educated and trained villagers were provided the ancient knowledge through the family lineage, while the villagers who had no direct connection to the ancient knowledge were the cultivators of the land. There was a place for everyone in the village, and there was value for what every individual produced for the good of the entire village. Leemel received an education that would prepare him to be a keeper of the scrolls or to be able to write inscriptions onto the temple walls for ancient records.

Anxiety began to set in as Leemel thought of leaving the city to continue the search for truth or the place that would provide the truth. Why was it necessary for people to abandon a city that they fought for against invading tribes? Was it necessary to walk away from the city built from everyone's sweat, the lakebed emptied to build the great gardens, temples, and a city that had provided a haven for over two hundred thousand people?

"Have the others who live to the north of us been asked to leave their homes and begin a similar journey?" Leemel asked the elder.

"Yes, we have all been asked to renew our search. Long before our time in Aztlán, it was prophesized that we would wander the earth searching for the truth until the new millennium, in the year 2050."

The elder stood as if to walk away, then observed, "Leemel, you have been given the gift of writing in the ancient knowledge, but in that writing, you have also been given the ability to learn what has been revealed to the ancient priests. You must learn to interpret the message of the gods to the priests. Use what is made available to you to guide yourself toward the truth that evades us all. But always remember that you are from Aztlán and that our way of life is inside of you, a part of your spirit always. You are one of the people chosen to wander, toil on the land to live, and learn from the pain you experience to learn of the gift of life that is hidden from the heat of the sun and the darkness of the seven caves."

Leemel's family lived in the southernmost part of the village lands where the tribes of Aztlán had been settled for over 300 years. Now, the family was faced with whether to leave a place they had always known as home or remain with those who would choose not to follow the advice of their spiritual leaders to begin their journey in pursuit of a greater truth. Leemel felt sadness in his heart as he realized that the time would soon come when his family would face the decision and that it would break the family apart. He knew that not all the family would choose to leave. All he could do was carry on with daily life as if nothing would change and hope that the truth of the prophecy would become a reality, and that life would remain as it was.

On a sunny early morning, Leemel and his family made their way through the jungle. The women ahead of him wore brightly colored bandanas wrapped around their heads as they carried their gatherings of corn, bananas, and freshly ground harina de maize to the market. These monthly trips to the market helped them earn extra money to trade for things the family could not grow or make. Their survival was only possible as long the family together worked the land when the weather allowed, and the gods provided a bountiful gift of precious food that could be sold or traded. The trading brought jewelry, animals for meat and milk, or cloth for dresses and shirts or bandanas. What they made from these things would be traded later.

Life was simple. At the end of the harvest, people rested and used it as a time for sacrifice and worship. A sacrifice to the sun god for a bountiful harvest was usually a small farm animal such as a baby goat (cabrito). The cabrito was sliced at the throat and bled until the sun required no further nourishment for the spirits. Once the worshiping had been completed, they built a great fire and barbecued the sacrifice for a family gathering. The family talked about the dreams that delivered them from the past and those that would carry us into the future.

Family treks through the jungle to the city were frequent, but the most important were these monthly journeys to the market. The day-to-day life would be difficult without those trips for supplies that could not be found in the jungle. Yes, life was difficult, but the forest always provided the necessities. There seemed to always be enough corn for tortillas and tamales with mangos or bananas to supplement their needs. Most of the family looked forward to the trip and the marketplace.

Irineogod'se youngest of the family and bursting with the new energy of a young jungle cat, was the first to notice the enormous pyramid that stood above the tree tops as a testament to the belief in the kings' ability to communicate with the gods and the relationship of faith the people of the Valley had with their gods faith that the gods would provide abundant harvests and healthy children and would guide each person's voyage into the outer worlds. As they walked out of the forest, they entered the city with its smooth roads made of stone squares leading to the market that was in the center of the square guarded by two temples for worship and ceremonies.

The temples stood as the sentinels for the city, protecting the citizens from what had been written in prophecy and which would soon come to stagnate the Indian way of life for the next eight hundred years. This way of life would not last forever, as most of the Indians had been taught. There would come a time when the people would have to consider the survival of the race over the continuation of life in the royal cities, they had built with their labor to acclaim a way of life.

The prophecy foretold the coming of a man with pale skin and hair that looked as if it were on fire. This foreign invader would arrive on a floating temple with immense white wings that pulled it on the waters, a temple that could race across the water, bringing with it many other pale-faced men, many with hair on their faces, hiding their intent. They would resemble an army ready for battle or an invasion ready to plunder the riches of the people and the land. Unknown to the people, this arrival would change their way of life, which would end, and they would be forced to abandon their cities. The foreigners would be experienced in destruction. They would know how to disarm our spiritual leaders with gifts, gestures, and words of foreign social and cultural beliefs.

When the time came, our ancient knowledge would be left behind. We left everything, including the city that served as our protector. We would then belong to a universe of knowledge, and collectively that knowledge would guide our spirits with the understanding that time would be our protector. We understood that we would survive the invasion and that our tribe would be reborn many centuries into the future.

CHAPTER 9
The Mix of Old and New Worlds

Pareces como una Mosca en la Leche.
(You look like a fly in milk.)
~ Dicho

Some might call it a mix of races and others a precautionary melting pot, but my father instinctively understood the danger of forgetting the origins of our birth. When I brought my blonde-haired, blue-eyed girlfriend home to him, my father said that I looked like a fly in milk. It seemed to him that I was getting closer and closer to the White world. He told me and my sibling's stories and left a trail of breadcrumbs for us to follow as a constant reminder of our place of origin.

The descendants of Aztecs are by birth warriors, explorers, artists, writers, scientists, and healers of varied backgrounds, and we are not willing to give that up. We used our family campfire stories—more on that in a future chapter—to preserve who we are and where we come from. We are people who understand that we are only a small part of this earth and that many other pieces fit together to make up our destiny and determine when it is our time. When the time arrives, we will know what to do. Our time seems near, which is why I am reflecting on my thoughts as the ancient writers used to. I sense the urgency of inscribing the past and the present and always looking to the future.

***

Once we left as a people tied to the pyramids of the sun and moon that served as our temples, our destiny was to wait until the earth was cleansed before we would return to our homelands with a piece of new knowledge, to revive what had been preserved for the new time, and to have a clearer understanding of the universe.

One of these visits by a foreigner to the center of the Indian world changed our family's destiny. On the last visit by the invaders, they touched the hand that made the first contact a forced destiny. This new destiny would introduce an ancient world to a new world that was experiencing its birth in a war against our people over the riches of the earth. The inner struggle of the land and its people began with the invasion of the foreigners, bringing their religion, values, and diseases that would begin the dilution of the people who populated the ancient world.

This newly created world brought men with hair the color of fire, of corn silk, and others who could have come from the same tribe as ours with black hair. Their eyes were distant, empty, lacking the light of the spirit, and of many colors: brown like the land to the north, green like the forest we lived in, blue like the waters that had no end, and dark eyes like ours. The strongest of the new men removed their hair from their heads and placed it on their faces. Their heads were smooth and shiny except around the base of the skull, and their hairy faces displayed only their eyes, like a warrior's mask. The hairless ones were usually the leaders for the other angry ones.

These strange men did not travel with their families. They traveled without their wives or companions of any kind. Men such as these could not have had much love in their hearts traveling without someone to share their inner selves. They could not share their thoughts, and they had no one to give them advice with which to make spiritual decisions. Without families or companions, they could not belong to or have a village. They were empty souls who knew nothing about the sun that nourished all life or the corn that gave everyone sustenance to the body and soul. It is possible that the emptiness of their spirits allowed them to commit acts of atrocities against a people without fear of offending the gods.

It was not clear why they had come except for what had been passed on by messengers who traveled from other regions. The reports came that these men were terribly angry people capable of brutality against other human beings without any religious purpose. Within the hearts of these men was the ability to kill for the jewelry worn by the men, women, and children of our world. How could such brutality exist? What value could be placed on a necklace, bracelet, or metal that glistened with the reflective colors of the sun? What would be worth the soul of an Indian spirit?

Indian Spirit

Black strands of obsidian,

Razor sharp,

Cutting through the wind.

Ancestors whisper at your shadow,

Defy the sun.

Black strands of obsidian,

Razor sharp,

Cutting through the wind.

Ancestors whisper at your shadow,

Ancient Sun Queen the successor.

Black strands of obsidian,

Razor sharp,

Cutting through the wind.

Ancestors whisper at your shadow,

Possessing ancestral blood of dignity.

Black strands of obsidian,

Razor sharp,

Cutting through the wind.

Ancestors whisper at your shadow,

Holding cities in the palm,

Of your hands,

Black strands of obsidian,

Razor sharp,

Cutting through the wind.

Ancestors whisper at your shadow,

Giving life to the walking dead.

The murderous acts of the men we came to know as Spaniards were brutal, committed with metal objects that could not be realized in time to protect those who might survive. Like locusts sweeping through a field and eating everything in their path, these invading warriors, without honor or respect for themselves, destroyed everything they came across.

Our people had expected the arrival as told in the prophecy. This invasion of men with their hair on fire from the evil side of the waters was anticipated by the wise, those who listened to the wisdom of the ages. Now, they were faced with the infiltrator's mission to destroy our religion and convert our world into one they could use to conquer others. It was also foretold that they would come to gather gold and precious stones for their leaders who had sent them in the first place and use our people for their personal needs. They took women from the villages by force, raped them, and enslaved others to gather more raw gold. They were never interested in jewelry, artistry, but only the raw metal that made the jewelry.

They came alone and had no one to hold them to account. They destroyed an entire civilization that received them with open arms without a reckoning from their families, who would never know of their atrocities—the terrible wrong done to innocents and undeserved brutal treatment. These men would never have to explain to their children why they murdered children or explain to their wives why they raped Indian women and produced mestizo offspring. These men possessed a purity of evil in their hearts that would survive through eternity. We need to remind ourselves that this happened once, and it could happen again.

Anger, hatred, and resentment swelled throughout the land toward these men with hair on their faces. Anger flourished and grew as they abused the trust of entire villages by kidnapping the greatest of the Indian women leaders, women with the strongest spirits and most extensive knowledge of our world to use for their pleasures and as advisors in conquering our world. Our people did not understand the depth of the foreigner's depravity, the invaders with different colored eyes and hair who would destroy the world we knew. We had no idea that this evil was hardwired into this enemy, the soldiers with eyes that reflected the sky but could not usher the beauty of the sky into their souls.

These soldiers ignored the strength of our family ties. They did not respect the strength of our religion that had maintained the unity of our civilization for longer than memory stood. They had no way of knowing that their visit was temporary and that they could never conquer the Aztec spirit that existed long before they had conceived the notion of making ships. They were unaware, while traveling on top of the water to faraway lands, that Mayan and Aztec families had been present in this world before the pyramids were built.

Once the women of the villages were taken away, some of the mestizo children followed. Some remained and were assimilated into our culture and worldview. We believed that more than one life on Earth guided our civilization. The strength of the family, according to the gods who guided the people who had been conquered, would forever remain. We were willing to accept new people into our world and mourned the children who followed the conquistadors as they pillaged each village that came into their path with each rumor of gold, silver, gems, or anything of value. Their pursuit was for wealth in the present with no concern for the past and no vision for the future.

The Spaniards never realized that they had changed their homeland forever by stealing the youngest, brightest, and most beautiful women and producing children. As they returned home, a new people emerged with the skin, hair, and eyes of the conqueror but with the Indian soul. The mestizo children brought a vision of the New World and a loyalty to the old. With their births came a new race that infiltrated the Spaniards, just as the Spaniards had infiltrated the original Indians. Thus, the Spaniards had condemned their own claim to a pure bloodline destiny. They became Aztec, unknowingly.

Veleela

If you recall the story of Leemel, his family would soon be the victim of one of those raids when the conquerors came in friendship to eat their food and share conversations with the entire family. They betrayed what had been shared by taking a piece of the family spirit, the oldest of the three daughters named Veleela. She was kidnapped without warning, without permission, and without letting anyone know where they would take her. How could such people be so evil as to accept friendship and hospitality and still splinter a family in the blink of an eye?

Families throughout the land were faced with the threat of this invader stealing their daughters for their pleasure and had no way of fighting the sticks that spit out fire and balls of metal that killed our warriors instantly. The Spaniards dressed in metal clothing with hats that could not be pierced by simple Indian spears of wood and stone. As a nation, we were no match for the warriors that came from across the waters. It was even less likely that individual families could raise their weapons against the well-armed, well-trained soldiers from Spain.

These conquerors were warriors made for battle, trained to perform acts of evil without guilt or remorse. They possessed the capacity to destroy an entire village, which gave shelter to the families of the women they had taken as wives without understanding or caring about the pain of their atrocity. One conquistador explained to a group of Indians gathered in the market that their invasion and acts of war were justified because they were bringing the word of God. He said that it was their duty to spread the word of their God through the Queen of Spain because she had been placed on the throne through an act of God. But what kind of God would permit the killing of women and children and the pillaging of villages for no reason whatsoever?

Who was this queen who caused families to be separated, and their homes destroyed? Veleela was taken from Leemel's family, and that destiny would affect us all. Leemel knew he'd never see her again, but also knew the Aztec gods chose her to go out into this new millennium to gather knowledge and return it to our civilization. The year reconning, according to our calendar, would be 2050. Then we'd welcome the new beginning, and the Indians of Aztlán would regain the ancient lands that belonged to the Aztecs.

Veleela was sent to learn of the New World and pass on the same charge to her children, requiring that they carry the message and pass it on to their children. And thus, so long ago, the campfire stories of my youth came to be. Thanks to the ancients, we had been taught through the generations that a return to their lands would signal their rebirth. Every one of ancient blood would begin to return with the accumulated knowledge gathered over the centuries of wandering. They would arrive to build a new civilization capable of withstanding any future invasion. Revival of the ancient lands would bring with it a greater knowledge of the farmlands and their relationship with the environment. The accumulated knowledge would also return commerce with merchants and reopen markets at the foot of the pyramids once again. It would be 800 hundred years before families began to return.

The Vasquez Family

Through Leemel's family's first contact with his sister Veleela and ten generations later, we became a mix of Spanish, Aztec, and ancient Mayan blood, a contradiction between the past and future generations for the family given the name Vasquez. Anyone who casually dips into the name Vasquez will learn it's one of the earliest forms of hereditary surnames derived from the Basque word "Bela" (meaning crow). The first Vasquez families originated in the Castile region of Spain.

As my forebears entered the twentieth century and reached the heights of European and Anglo education, we maintained some of the ancient ways without knowing that they had already been instilled in us to carry on from generation to generation. We passed on the stories and continued our rituals around our campfires; we practiced herbal healing and sometimes dark natural healing. Our medicine was what we used first, and when we did not know what medicines would work, as a last resort, we would use Anglo medicine.

Many families took on some of the ancient names of plants and animals as a reminder of where we came from, why we are here, and what we reflect. In the northern part of Spain, the Vasquez was known as a family of adventurers, explorers with hearts that could freeze in the middle of tropical summer. Life was to be grabbed from the sky and squeezed until its breath became solidified with the pressures of the next adventure. The moment was for living, and the future was for others to contemplate and plot the outcomes of what would eventually be today.

Since the time of separation, our families have wandered the world, and it was understood that the lineage of people with Indian blood, the ones who remained with the tribal people's blood in their veins, would be the carriers of the knowledge I spoke of earlier, passed on by the artists, healers of natural medicines, priests, warriors, and writers. They would explore the future and flourish through the offspring who came from the first Indian bearing the first child who came to be known as a Mexican of today, the people of the people, La Raza.

La Raza

La Raza has evolved out of the careful blending of foreign blood, culture, and race. La Raza is the offspring of the Aztec and Mayan worlds and the people who inter-married to disguise the next step in the advancement of civilization. The awakening would come through wandering the world accumulating knowledge from other worlds to be offered to the spirits of the great temples, and the pyramids in the middle of the city that we had to abandon but that would still be standing centuries later.

While many of our people have searched for the answers the world over, looking for the answers to the questions that have no relevance, we have been hidden from destruction. As a new people created through acts of brutality, we have been sent out to learn from our conquerors and to accumulate knowledge that would be returned to the villages and tribes to protect those who stayed behind. Many stayed behind to face hunger, guarding the temples of our ancient priest who had the power to grant us our names, which have been forgotten since our departure, names such as El Pajaro, El Coyote, and La Vivora. These names were given to us by the priest who laid out the design of who we would be and where we would fit in the world.

Note that we assimilated to a large degree where we were sent. We even sent our children into wars that were not ours to remind ourselves that we are warriors in a pure and brutal sense. We are warriors who do not require bullets, bombs, or chemicals. We are warriors, relying on common sense, unity, strength, intelligence, and the spirit gods. We do not forget the valor of the past and the sacrifice that needed to be made. Our young men and women volunteered to go to distant battles for the sake of gaining knowledge, preserving our history, and serving as a living legacy of the ancient ones. Death was just another vehicle to enter the next world and observe what had been accomplished and what would come next.

The greatest fear we had as youth was the fear of failing the elders and not arriving at our destinies. Some we lost in the journey of transition from the old race. The lost ones chose to pursue an identity that could never be achieved, the effort to become a mirror image of the conqueror, the Anglo. In the pursuit of becoming Anglo, our youth lost the gift of Indian strength and could never arrive at the threshold of becoming a complete being. The color of their skin, eyes, hair, and the way that they viewed the world kept them from becoming Anglo. Instead of becoming something else, they lost everything.

The people of the ancient land were lost in more ways than one. They were geographically lost but had also lost faith in knowing the destiny that awaited all of us. They forgot to seek answers. They were not sent to the new world to assimilate but to learn and return with the knowledge of the ancient priests. It was not our mission to become accepted and settle for eternity in a world that contradicts the survival of humanity. Some were lost in the transition due to the power of that greed that grips all people. Some we lost because of temptation from the physical world that could not be overcome without the closeness of an ancient family.

I find it fascinating, honoring, and a grave responsibility that this story of survival and rebirth has come to me. I'm constantly amazed that our civilization left their homes without a blueprint or road map. They had lived in ancient lands from the beginning of time but departed for a new world with only their wits and faith, not even knowing how to return. The only guide was the instinct of ancient ancestors and the help of the new knowledge and the Anglo side. Perhaps not only their mindset, but their physical bodies made it easier for some to tolerate our migration to the new world.

The following paragraphs might help readers internalize the backstory of La Raza. The imposed new blood brought rewards as well as an internal conflict to La Raza. We have the constant struggle of maintaining the Indian roots of our existence and living with the blood of the conquerors. We are a people that have come to terms with who we are: of two worlds, one that was imposed on us through conquest and violence, the other that will guide us into our new existence. We recognize that we possess blood that was not of our choosing. It was forced on us, but the other blood of ancient ways with ancient cities, knowledge, and a written history has always been a part of us and the Spanish never managed to destroy all of it. It still exists.

People who choose to recognize themselves as La Raza have accepted the internal conflict, and while Anglo blood flows through veins, they allow their Indian blood to guide their lives. The Indian prophecy predicted that from the conquest, a new race would be born, a people that would combine the language, customs, and religion of the conqueror with the ancient ways of the tribes. The crucifix, the Christian symbol that the Spaniards wore around their necks, would eventually be adapted. Our people found some similarity in symbolism to the four destructions and new beginnings that came from water, wind, fire, and sun.

We had always known that the gods dwelled in those places who created the earth, the land that we thrived on, that nourished our world with water, spreading the seeds of the jungle with its great winds and fire to cleanse itself of the unwanted. We had always been guided by the symbol of the four directions, with an understanding of our place. This made it easy for the Indian world to tolerate the foreign religion, and it was natural to informally accept the sign of the cross as it meant one thing to the Spaniards and another to the Indians.

Life in this world for the Indian soul would be lost without these directions. For us, the top of the cross points to the north, which is always associated with the color black, to the south with blue, right to the east with red, and to the west with white. Each sun marked a different time on the land. The coming and going of each new sunrise marked the beginning of change. The changes were sometimes created by the destruction of the sun by a wild beast, a hurricane, a fire, a flood, or tribal turmoil. The conquista came to the land and ushered in a time for a new sun, a time of waiting for the new sun to rise, and a time to flourish with the epoch.

La Raza—People of the New Sun

Vibrant sounds, echoes, bounding from the forest
floor reaching its canopy of trees.

Jungle sounds, life repeated, tree to tree reaching
the sky, dream captured.

Brilliant sun, serpent gods, night sky prophesies,
crossroads, future demands,

Pyramid's shadows shade, humid walk, a path to

the new world.

Forgotten language, people speak in silence,
hidden among the stone walls.

Hair-covered faces, blue, green eyes, invaders,
animals carry a burden.

Metal spears, silver bladed long knives, swords,
exploding sticks, chaos!

Stars announced, premonition of arrival,
prophesy, riding on beasts of burden.

Destruction! Purposeless, without intention,
without consequence, without understanding.

We were there, in an early life, bearing witness
awaiting, destiny of our children.

Genocidal Invaders, cultural rejection,
intervention of a civilization, destruction!

Families broken, in peril, daughters, sisters,
mothers, imposed unions.

Indian blood flows, alien collision, new blood,
new people, new race,

Raza is Born!

Destiny, walking, on earth mother, original
peoples, in conflict,

Alien blood, running through Brown and White
bodies, black, blond, red hair.

Abandoned jungle, stone temples, halls of
learning, abandoned halls, a new beginning.

Tribal cities once for hundreds of thousands left
for the rebirth, awakening.

New people new journey begins.

Mothers, fathers, brothers, sisters, separated,
mixed blood, cultures collide.

Gods, ceremonies, rituals, challenge the past,
forging a future.

Ancient knowledge, wisdom, hidden, guarded,
isolated, exploitation, avoided.

Civilization abandoned, opal-shaped eyes look
north, ancient spirits wander.

Cities abandoned, human spirit embraces natural
world, earth, water, wind, fire.

Land, water, nourish, a people, wandering,
seeking knowledge, assimilation.

Tribes of colors, born Black, Brown, White.
Languages merge, wisdom grows.

Knowledge multiplies, we become, names
change, vision evolves, discovery, Expansion,
ancient tribal lands, rediscovered, origins, water,
rivers, food, people, return.

Generations north accumulated, science, art,
humanity, land, water, air.

Learning, living, exploring, evolving, a new race is
born, new cities, villages, north.

Souls of the past, spirits of the future, await, a

new millennium, we wait for the time.

Modern cities, on ancient stones, roads over
original paths, old dreams, revisited.

We gather, cities filled, people of many colors,
languages form many worlds.

Yesterday, community festivals, modern city,
modern people, I heard.

Ancient story, in ancient tongue with knowledge
of the hidden knowledge

The time has come, we have become a new
people, new color, world knowledge.

We have become Raza! The new race of all
people!

We are home in our land, the prophecy has
arrived!

***

Following the Mexican Revolution, cultural philosopher José Vasconcelos penned the essay "La Raza Cósmica," or "The Cosmic Race," in 1925 in response to white supremacist rhetoric coming out of the United States and Europe. Vasconcelos argued that a "fifth race" of people had emerged in the Americas that encompassed races from around the world and transcended all the others.

The mixture of the Indigenous and the Old World, he wrote, were "the moral and material basis for the union of all men into a fifth universal race, the fruit of all the previous ones and amelioration of everything past."

I chose to be Raza. Many of my Vasquez relatives are Raza.

The Spanish brought us the means to travel into the new world. They brought a language accepted at the time, a government, artificial money, and a need to explore other worlds. My spirit has always been Indian of the ancient land and Mejicano from the mixed blood or mestizo. To be mestizo is to be Raza and to be Raza is to possess the Indian spirit and be part of an infinite plan.

Mestizo

A mestizo is born, destined, ancient prophecy.

Conquest, foreign invaders, red hair, blue eyes,

Unknown language, rituals on their knees,
symbols, the four destructions

Forever! Change, chaos, turmoil, oppression,
captivity.

Red eyes in the dark of night, glowing like hot
coals,

Raging pain, taken, mothers, wives, sisters,

Birth follows, secrets created, invaders claim the
forbidden.

Children raised, rebellion grows, resistance
inspired.

New world, begins heartbeats pounding, sounds
bursting.

Flowing streams of tears pushed downward.

Rose colored cheeks moistened with sorrow.

Voices clash in objection as they break.

A black mirrored night, shattering to dust.

A mestizo child was born in conflict and resistance.

CHAPTER 10
An Impressionable Young Mind

Podrán cortar todas las flores pero no podrán detener la primavera.
(You can cut all the flowers, but you can't stop the spring.)
~Pablo Neruda

This seems like the perfect place to segue back into my early years of traveling north from the borderlands of Texas to places with names such as Wenatchee, Mabton, Hermiston, Echo, Stanfield, and Payette. It seemed like an adventure before I started school, and I've described all the preparations and packing up with my aunts and uncles during this time—which, in hindsight, was challenging and sometimes brutal. And yet, my overall impression as a child was that these were happy times.

There was always music in the background, laughing, joking, an occasional debate, and decisions about what food needed to be prepared and how it could be preserved for the four-day trip. The preparations for the summer harvest stirred excitement because of the anticipation of going to new places, seeing people who were not like us, and being able to observe from the safety of our car a deer dash across the highway or a coyote dashing from the roadside once they heard us approach or the rattlesnake in the middle of the road.

I remember the first time we saw a rattlesnake on the road, and my father was so careful not to run it over. He immediately turned around, making a U-turn, with his wheels driving over the creature without hitting it. In complete surprise, I asked my father why he did that, and he answered that it was bad luck to cross a rattlesnake's path without going over one more time for good luck on our voyage.

As I thought about why we had to travel back and forth from our Texas home to the northern states, I was reminded of the ancient stories of the migration from the seven caves to the interior of what is now Mexico and that there would come a time when our people would leave to learn about the land beyond their villages, to gain new knowledge, languages, culture, and people. It struck me that we had become a part of the prophecy. We were living what had been foretold.

While traveling from our home in Eagle Pass, it was evident that we were leaving a place that would be foreign to the many people we would meet along the way. Where we lived, it was common to see cacti from the living room window. The shade in our yard provided by mesquite trees with everything brown from lack of water created a dry powdery dirt with a fine powder texture. We were leaving a place where Spanish was the common spoken language. It did not matter where we went in Eagle Pass; everyone spoke Spanish. We could go to city hall, a gas station, or a grocery store and all we heard was Spanish. It was rare that we would hear any English spoken and even more rare to see any Anglos, and when we did, they spoke Spanish.

Traveling North, we could gradually see the change in scenery as we drove west from El Paso. From dry rocky land with cactus, mesquite, and dry brown desert soil, we eventually passed California's many green orchards and vineyards. We arrived in the region where they grew the biggest strawberries I had ever seen. One of the most beautiful parts of our migration was driving through northern California, where I saw the tallest trees, I had ever seen—as tall as some of the mountains in Texas.

As we began to drive into Oregon, we could see more of this gradual change. The trees were still tall but not giants. There were large fields of seed grass, wheat, and Christmas trees. I remember thinking this would be a wonderful place for a kid like me to live. It would be like living in a wonderland. Our migration north was not just a change in scenery; it was a journey to places that introduced us to different food, language, and mannerisms.

Oh, and then there was the language. English was the only language other than when we would meet the occasional Mexican family that had settled in the north. Some who lived in these places made me feel unwelcome, as I've mentioned before. They had a colder nature than the people from Eagle Pass, and I felt that they were not as receptive to us and that they did not want to spend much time around us. Our migrations from town to town exposed us to people who treated us as people who would only be there to do their work, to harvest the seasonal crop, and in a few weeks, we would be gone.

We would only be there temporarily and there would be no time to establish relationships. After all, we always knew that this was not our home and in a few months we would return. Many of the Mexican families that settled North had been there for several generations. Their families were some of the early arrivals who went there to support the miners or to mine for themselves, to buy land and farm the fertile soil that was just now being revealed. There were many who left Mexico to lead the mule trains that supplied the sprouting towns, to supply the miners mostly in California but also in parts of Oregon and Idaho; some traveled north to establish their own businesses.

It was typically the mestizos who traveled north to escape the rule of the Spanish and wait for the time that it would be theirs, those who believed the prophecy and understood that one day, whether it was during their time or after their lifetime, that the land they stood on would become part of the Aztlán once again.

Our evenings were a time to gather around the usual campfire, where sometimes Tia Rico would gather the family to share events or stories that often times were designed to pass down learning and knowledge to the young people that possessed the endurance to last the evening late into the night.

One evening, one of the youngest in the crowd, a young boy who was known for his curiosity and endless questions—me—began his curious pursuit to understand why some Mexican families lived in places where it was rare to find families like ours. In other words, I wanted to understand the history of permanent migration. These Hispanics began staying up north many decades ago. Why had they stayed and not migrated back home? Why didn't they go back like we did? What kind of work do they do in the winter?

My uncle Andres, whose nickname was Conejo (Rabbit), a name given to him because he could run so fast, looked at me and explained that these families stayed behind to get things ready for when we came back to do the harvest work. He told him the families had not planned to stay but did so for a chance to work year-round on farms, even though these northern places seemed like a foreign country to us.

Later, I learned many Mexicans who migrated to the territories of California and the southern tip of what is now Oregon never intended to become American citizens. California had been Indian land, then a Mexican territory when they migrated north, and later became a U.S. territory long after their arrival. Their settlements had been established 150 years before the arrival of the Europeans. It was never a conscious decision for the early Mexican settlers to become Americans. America came to them by force, and their children and grandchildren were born into U.S. citizenship.

Yet well into the fourth and fifth generations, Mexican descendants still had a stronger connection to Mexico's history, language, and culture than to the American culture, especially along the border states Arizona, California, New Mexico, and Texas.

There was no real American culture in my family for several generations, from the time of the early settlement until California became a state and more Europeans began to settle in the West and Southwest. The new settlements brought changes that influenced the culture through an eagerness to expand. Europeans brought with them a need to create laws that altered the Mexican influence forever and set a new course for an area previously occupied by our Indian ancestors and then by the Mexican culture, religion, and the Spanish language.

Before the arrival of the Europeans, the schools taught all their classes in Spanish until they began to arrive in larger numbers and at a greater pace, at which time the existing Mexican territorial government chose to provide bilingual education and taught classes in English. As more Europeans began to arrive, it was only a matter of time until all classes were being given in English, and the Mexicans who could afford it pulled their children from public schools and sent them to private Spanish-speaking schools.

It has always puzzled me why the Anglos disliked us so much. Sometimes I go out of my way to make excuses to feel better and not have to try to understand the nature of why human beings feel that way when they appear to need, want, and have the same things I do. What was different about my family and the people we knew was our different history, language, and culture. Even more apparent…we were not light skinned. We came in colors that might pass as Anglo to light Brown to Black. It only took a slight difference to draw such a negative response from the communities we traveled to for work.

The Black Legend

I have a faint memory of a campfire gathering at my grandparents' where the discussion focused on the Spaniards and what they had done and what it meant to the way of life of our ancestors. Whenever they described the crimes committed against our people, it was tied to the La Leyenda Negra or "The Black Legend," which meant nothing to me at the time. There somehow seemed to be a connection to the Black Legend and how they thought we were viewed in the Anglo world. The most common of all excuses is that they don't understand us and that they are afraid of our language and customs. Their fear of the unknown made them act in desperation with hate in their hearts, or has it been hatred for a perceived race of people who are not like them? It has been difficult accepting the idea that a group of people would hate us because of the color of our skin or that we were from Mexico and, worse yet, that we might be Catholic.

The Black Legend is a term used to describe a distorted, negative image of Spain and Spanish people who originated during the 16th century and was perpetuated by other European countries during the 17th and 18th centuries. The Black Legend asserts that Spanish people and Spanish colonial rule were cruel, oppressive, and religiously intolerant. The Black Legend has been used to justify wars and imperialistic policies, as well as to create a false image of Spanish culture.

It was as if being American and living this way of life included having someone to blame for their lack of success or feeling like they were superior to any person or group of people who were different than them. We always seemed to run into hateful people as we traveled looking for work. It was typical to run into someone working in the gas station, restaurant, or store who disliked us as a people without even speaking to us. There would be the greeters standing out in front of the entrances to downtown or near a tavern waiting to start something with any innocent person who appeared vulnerable.

My family and the other families we met in the fields and camps were part of a group of people that got stuck with labels like "migrant worker," "spic," "greaser," "wet back," and sometimes "fish eaters" because we were Catholic. These labels stuck and often conjured many notions and ideas or reactions from community people and sometimes from governments, For example, the origins of the derogatory "wet back" that gained popularity and became part of the racist playbook originated from a government immigration program that was officially called "Operation Wetback," implemented by Joseph Swing, the Director of the United States Immigration and Naturalization Service (INS). The program launched in June 1954 by U.S. Attorney General Herbert Brownell.

Oregon was a state that we tried to avoid because the farmers were notorious for not having housing for farm workers. They also had a reputation for announcing more work than existed, which caused us to travel to places that could not provide enough work for all those families that made the journey. Being able to know that we could work the entire summer with little to no downtime was crucial for a comfortable life when we returned to our homes in Eagle Pass. Everything depended on the money that would be saved after our expenses were covered. The rest would pay for the electricity, winter jackets, and sweatshirts for the children, and maybe some materials to buy insulation for the rooms that had been added to the house in the previous year. We built our homes one room and section at a time according to how much work was available and how much we could save.

Clinched Fists

The young man stood silent,

Friends with anger,

Fists clench,

Screaming at people,

Deaf to sounds of violence.

A young man's heart.

Struggles with paradox,

Fighting the days of dust in your eyes

With a hoe in your hand.

Your future has been decided.

By the past.

Your spirit drifts,

Ancestors harvesting corn,

Building the future,

Gathering knowledge,

Pitting your soul against itself.

In our migrations, we traveled through many small rural towns that seemed to all have the same bowling alleys, taverns, and movie theaters; everything seemed so familiar and consistent, yet different. For some reason, some communities were more receptive to our arrival than others. We noticed that the pace of small-town life was safe and comfortable. Some towns would only have one streetlight, and people would drive twenty miles per hour or less through the center of town. They would stop in the middle of the road to say hello to anyone they might have known, spotted walking along the sidewalk, and it seemed as if the same farmers owned the same farms across the country to us. Everyone seemed to look alike. As far as we could tell, every town always had the same people. They appeared the same, and their behavior toward us was the same: shouting insults and ignoring us when we needed services. Signs in Texas and Arizona displayed the Anglos' hatred for the Mexicans by announcing that no dogs or Mexicans would be served. In most cases, our people were denied entrance to public places such as restaurants and taverns.

It is hard to imagine how so much hatred could have grown in so many of the people who lived in these small, beautiful towns and who, in most cases, were recent arrivals themselves. Maybe it wasn't hatred; maybe it was a reaction to the unknown. After all we were the new people in town, and we were never in one place for too long. We spoke different languages. Some spoke Spanish and others the Indigenous language spoken of their tribal village. We listened to different music and were very expressive in the way we talked with each other. It is not uncommon to see us waving our arms in all directions during a normal conversation at a family barbecue. It's how we display our emotions. We are not only expressive in our mannerisms but, at times, can become very boisterous if the individual speaking comes from a big family. After all, it's the way of survival to be loud and self-minded if you come from a family of six or more. If you were not loud, you would never be heard.

The greatest personal pressure I felt up north (We would call it El Norte or the North) was the demand to assimilate. This was always the greatest driving force that allowed me to view myself in ways that made me feel the most comfortable and part of the larger society that would not welcome me into its womb unless I were a child of parents descended from the Pilgrims and spoke the same language. English was the only accepted language and culture. But to me, it was non-culture, or at least that is how I perceived it. How could I see it as a culture if it did not have healers who were both righteous and could spare people from the evil spells that could be cast over an entire family or make the ugliest of men attractive in the eyes of any woman?

How could people feel like a community if they did not have customs like the coming-out parties (quinceañeras) for the young women when they turned fifteen? It was difficult to understand how I could ever become part of a community if there were few opportunities to participate in the kinds of activities and events that I was used to enjoying. We could not see that there are ways to participate in personal interactions as an individual or with the family.

Of course, I could never become a child who could belong to this new world in a way that was expected of me. It was too late for me to be part of a non-culture; I had already been raised as a Mexican with an Indian spirit and the history of an ancient civilization, culture, language, and spirit. I would later realize how difficult it would be to struggle with acceptance without questioning my existence and considering the denial of the roots of my birth.

That rejection of my roots never became a reality because of the constant support I received from my family, reinforcing the importance of what was left for us to guard and protect. My father always reminded me of the pyramids that were left behind as a reminder that our return to the homeland was an eventuality. He would point to the south and talk of the time that he would return the legacy that was left waiting for the first of the family members to reclaim their inheritance. On one of our trip's homes, my father decided to take me to the pyramids outside of Mexico City, to Teotihuacan and the Pyramid of the Sun and the Pyramid of the Moon. As we walked through the complex, I imagined who had lived there and what they might have done for work or school or where the marketplace might have been.

I quickly found out that my father had taken me there for a purpose. He began to remind me that this was where we came from and that I was part of an ancient tribe that had created these monuments, and that the city had astronomers, architects, artists, craftspeople, and our own language and music. He said, "I want you to remember when we go back north that most of the people who curse us and call us names cannot show you a place like this and say, 'This is where you come from.'" This moment carved in stone deep in my inner spirit, what my identity would be from that day forward.

I went north from Mexico, but I was of Indian descent. In my heart, because of the stories of my elders, I always knew I was Indian, but this moment made it real. My dreams became about exploring the world in which my ancestors had wandered and discovering the writings of the ancients or producing artwork with the power and strength of the Aztecs. Their faces were my own; I could see myself in some of the ancient sculptures.

Many things kept me apart from those red, blond, and brunette-haired children, who oftentimes had blue, green, or hazel eyes, while almost everyone I know had dark brown eyes that were so dark they looked black and oval shaped due to my ancestral background, my color, and my language. Over time, I arrived at a philosophy that became my mantra in which I proclaimed that I shouldn't worry about those things that I couldn't change. After all, I still carried with me the color tones of the Aztecs that protected me from the ferocious sun, the jungle that had no mercy for those unprepared to fight for the worth of living. My black almond-shaped eyes with blue around the edges were a constant reminder that I was mestizo; my skin was caramel to match the earth, and the strands of my hair were black as obsidian like the stones of our weapons.

My identity was always on display and no mystery to those who came from the same civilization. No, there was never a time when I felt that assimilation had a grip, and I would be at risk of becoming part of the mainstream. In fact, the Anglos who lived near me wanted me to be mainstream, but why was it so important for me to be so much like them? Couldn't I fit into their world and remain who I was? Why was it unacceptable to have the best of both worlds and speak both languages (Spanish and English), and most of all, why weren't there more children like me?

My early lessons in this socialization process led me to believe that I could be accepted as a human being and eventually become a part of the community. We were taught that everyone was equal, and that America was the land of plenty with justice for all. It was never my intention to pursue equality or justice as a nine-year-old, but just the same it was something of immense importance in my learning process. I wanted to be the same as the White children who had nice homes, wore new clothes, spoke English without an accent, and arrived at school in brand new automobiles painted in the colors of the rainbow (occasionally, there would be a black car that always brought mystery).

With those early lessons, however, came a price tag that I could never afford. I would never pay the price of giving up the essence of being Mexican for the sake of being accepted in the Anglo world. I was born Raza and had known that from the beginning of my consciousness, and it was reinforced by my family and the campfire stories. The sounds of music, laughter, and the rhythmic melodies of the ancient tongues haunted my character. How could I abandon the centuries of knowledge and memory of my ancestors for the artificial acknowledgment of becoming some kind of Anglo which for me would be a contradiction?

As a community, we continued to hang onto many of our ancestral customs, religious practices, medicines, and ancient Indian languages. Beyond the challenge of our origins, we also came from the ranks of the poor and the working class, and we happened to possess the brown hues of the earth on our skin. Instead, desperation and a lifetime of fighting to survive was our destiny.

Our inheritance was the struggle that our ancestors left behind, and our only way out was to recognize there would be pressures to walk away from the past and immerse ourselves in the present. My personal choice was to become someone I had always been. Acceptance for me began when I awoke from the intoxication of those things that are purchased and not earned. I am Raza, and I have walked this earth with the gift of my ancestors and the legacy that they left behind.

Getting an education in the U. S. created an internal struggle of wanting to be like everyone else, haunted by the reality that the Indian blood in my veins, the color of my skin, and my connection to Mother Earth would keep me grounded.

The most difficult challenge I faced was going to through the American schools constantly facing the challenge of complete assimilation or finding the balance that allowed me to cling to my identity.

Maintaining the balance of who I am in a foreign culture has been difficult and sometimes tempting, but at seventy-four, I still cherish the thought of belonging to the world of the ancients.

CHAPTER 11
An Education

It was instilled in us that the only inheritance a poor family can leave is a good education.
(The first Latina to hold the post of President at Cal State Fullerton, the country's largest state university system.)
~ Mildred García

As children, in the schools in El Norte, we were taught from the time we entered kindergarten or elementary school that if we were good and obeyed all the rules, worked hard, and made it over the hurdles placed before us without giving up, we would be successful in the eyes of society. The acceptance of society would also open doors to wealth, security, and comfort. All we had to do is obey all the laws, believe in the Christian God, abandon the Indian ways, get a good American education, and speak English without an accent. I came to learn that, as a group, the expectation of inclusion did not apply to someone with Indian and Mexican roots and a last name that ended in a Z.

My first exposure to the Anglo people for extended periods was in the public-school systems of the Southwest and the West. This experience made me feel less than a human. From the first day of first grade, I remember ridicule about the color of my skin, which was often referred to as chocolate, and the straightness of my hair, which was long and black. The kids said that I had Indian hair, and in fact, it is Indian hair because I am mostly Indian.

In the schools along the Mexico border, it was difficult to spot an Anglo kid, and no one made comments about my hair, eyes, or language. When I finally went to a mostly all-White school, there were immediate comments about my skin color, hair, and eyes.

It felt like the constant criticism became a tool to attempt to control me and other Mexican kids like me. Every day I was called spic, wetback, or greaser by other children. The teachers referred to me and other Mexican kids as monos because we spoke only one language. It was difficult to understand that my teachers could watch these attacks on another human being, on a small child, and not react in any protective way. It was as if the teachers were giving permission to those children to be evil by not responding to their atrocities.

The thought of where my father came from was an enormous influence on me in accepting the day-to-day challenges of going to a school—the name-calling, isolation, and laughter that I could not understand. My father and his siblings grew up as orphans. As children they did not have the privilege of school as they had to work to provide food and to maintain the simple shack, they called a home. They did not have the luxury of thinking about going to school even as they came to realize the importance of getting an education to get better jobs.

The immediate need for daily living was always the priority for the household. Education for my father was not the priority, out of necessity, but his destiny was to never forget the importance of education, and he chose to pursue his general education diploma (GED) as an adult and finally achieve a four-year college degree at age sixty-five. My father's commitment to educating himself and watching him study in the evenings as a child left an imprint on me on the importance of education. I did not know that he was only studying for a GED; all I knew was that he was studying and that it was important.

My father wanted me to go to an Anglo school. I was too young to visualize that which came naturally to him. It was hard to imagine how my life would be different than it was at that moment and that it could be better by going to a school where no one spoke my language, where everyone was White, and where they didn't know anything about our way of life. The future could not take care of the anxiety I was feeling. It had been decided that we would try to stay in El Norte so that all of us could get an education in what was at that time an all-White school. As my father was looking into the school, we found out that there were only three Mexican families in the entire community and only one Mexican kid in my grade.

On the first day of class, I was waiting for the person who would be my teacher to come into the room. I had no sense of what to expect. My father and I stood in silence waiting and it seemed longer than the lifetime I had already lived before she finally appeared.

As she walked toward us, I could see that she was larger than any person I had ever seen before. She wore a blue dress with little white flowers smothering the dress. It seemed as if it was thrown over her like a dust cover over a couch to save the newness for a special day, maybe when company came to visit.

She stepped through the door and said, "Hello, my name is Mrs. Bauer."

I remember thinking that at least I could understand her greeting. Beyond her original introduction, it was difficult to figure out everything she discussed with my dad, although he smiled from time to time and nodded his head many times throughout the conversation. It all seemed as if I was watching a movie about someone I knew and not about my future or what would happen to me in this classroom.

Then, in an instant, my dad was gone, and there I was, sitting alone and staring at all those strange faces, surrounded by people that I was taught could not be trusted. After all, they had a reputation for being cold, unresponsive to human emotion, and unfriendly with a willingness to be cruel. Waiting for what destiny had brought me, I felt a coldness in the air from all the concrete structure held up by dull green walls and steel doors. It seemed as if the surroundings of the classroom were used to control opportunity and not a place for children to experience freedom. My education on how to become a good American would soon begin.

Before the other children arrived, I allowed the silence to receive my thoughts. I stood in silence, staring out the window and wishing I was going to work in the fields with everyone else. At least in the fields, the families knew me. They would watch over me and show me the love that fertilized my spirit. In the fields, I knew that they would speak my language, and we would understand each other. We would laugh at the same jokes and enjoy the same music and at lunch. savor the wonderful food. Thoughts of running away raced through my mind as I continued to stare out the window, hoping for a miracle that would never come.

The thought of my father leaving had not entered my mind until I saw him shaking hands with the teacher. Then I realized that he would soon be walking out the door, down the hall, and into the fields where I had worked only the day before. *God, what will I do if he leaves? He is the only reason I'm here.*

"Dad!" I yelled out as I stepped toward him. He smiled, walking toward me.

"Mijo," he said, "I have to go to work, and we will be back for you when you get out."

G*et out,* I was thinking. It was as if I was going to jail, and I had to get out to leave. How could I get out of this place before I had to spend even a day? Of course, that never happened, and the time finally came when I watched my dad leave.

Suddenly, I began to hear distant voices echoing, bouncing off the concrete walls, making sounds that I could not understand, like there were a hundred schoolteachers coming in my direction. How many teachers were out there, and what would they expect me to do once they got here? My mind was filled with so many questions, and my inner self was full of anxiety, wishing the day was over and I could be in the comfort of the shack that served as our temporary home. There was no way to get out of this situation that I was cornered into. I felt as if I had just been put into a cage, waiting for someone to determine what my fate would be. Of course, later I would come to realize that my early teachers had a hand in determining my fate, and they had a major influence on my early choices.

The first day of school was the same for many children, I now understand, but all I knew was that my first day became a day of fear, anxiety, and humiliation as the other children began to arrive and Mrs. Bauer began to talk with me. Of course, it was in English, and I could only pick up a few words. More children began to arrive. As I watched them interact with each other, it seemed like they knew each other. How I wished that I knew at least one of these kids that I could talk with and hide away in a corner and ignore everything that I could not understand. Standing alone in the middle of a room is the loneliest feeling I have ever had. Everyone was watching my every move down to my facial expressions.

Sitting in the classroom surrounded by children excited by the energy of entering a world where everyone except Mrs. Bauer was four feet tall, where our only purpose was to wait for recess and play, which was one thing that I could see we all had in common. There was so much fluid energy flowing through the classroom running like a wild stream touching each child except for me because I could not understand a single word they were saying. It was impossible to understand why a kid would break out into laughter, followed by other children starting to laugh. If only I could become a part of that activity. All I could think about was waiting for the end of the day and going to the comfort of home.

Eventually, the moment arrived when Mrs. Bauer yelled out, "Everyone, please sit down." Everyone knew exactly what to do. I stood there for what seemed to be hours until I decided to pick a desk to sit at; unfortunately, it was in the front of the classroom. Mrs. Bauer moved up front as well and began talking with every word in English. My only wish was for her not to look at me or ask me any questions because I knew that I would not be able to understand. God must have ignored my prayer because suddenly, she walked up to me and started talking to me in English, and I couldn't comprehend a single word. Horror set in, and I felt an overwhelming urge to run out of the classroom into the field behind the school and hide there until school let out.

Running away was not possible, though, because my father sat with me the night before, talking with me for hours, telling me the importance of education and how I would appreciate the knowledge I'd gain. He talked about how important it was for me to learn English. He wanted me to have a better education than he received. But all I could think about was being able to lie down and go to sleep. How important could it be for a six-year-old Mexican kid whose only friends and family spoke nothing but Spanish?

Suddenly, I realized that Mrs. Bauer was still standing in front of me, staring into my eyes, waiting for a response to words that had no meaning to me. I just sat there with my head bowed down, looking toward the floor as a sign of respect, like we were taught to give to adults. Abruptly she grabbed me by the chin, pulled my face up, and stared into my eyes as if she was expecting me to answer the question. I didn't know whether to run or hold my ground and take whatever would come my way. Fear provided the answers to my reaction. I was too afraid to get up and run away so I just sat there until she let go of my chin and began to walk away as the other children broke out into a chorus of laughter. How could I survive this humiliation? Everyone was laughing at me, and they had to be thinking that I was dumb.

If only these children knew that I could not speak English. Or would it even matter? As far as I could tell, there was no one who could speak Spanish. If there was one person, then I would know someone who could discover that I liked to do the same things that they liked to do. How could they learn to speak Spanish, and why hadn't my family taught me English? The first questions about who I am and where I came from began to form. Most important of all, it was the first time that I began to question why my father had not prepared me for something. How could he send me to school so unprepared? If only these children could speak Spanish, they would know that I traveled all over the country, lived in many unusual places, had different jobs, and made money to buy my school clothes. If only they could speak Spanish.

Finally, the end of my first day came, and it seemed like I had spent a lifetime waiting for the final bell to ring, giving me permission to go home to people who loved me and could understand my language. As I stepped out of the classroom, I wondered about Gerardo. My one-year-older brother had never attended an American school and had started his first day of second grade. What must he have gone through? Was it the same thing or was it just my weakness?

As I walked toward the place where we agreed to meet, I spotted Gerardo. He began to smile. He was glad to see me. If I could have seen myself, I would have seen the same kind of smile on my face. We greeted each other like adults having a family reunion after years of not seeing each other. Then we were silent for quite a while. My dad was not able to come to get us, so we decided to walk home. Finally, I built up the nerve to ask, "How was it?"

He stopped in mid-step, turned to look at me, and began talking, the words pouring from his mouth like water from a fountain. It was as if he had been waiting for anyone to ask the question or just to have an ear willing to listen. "They couldn't understand a word I was saying. Every time I said anything, the other kids laughed and pointed at me as if I were some kind of idiot. I can't go back to that school. Those kids are the meanest people I have ever met. The teacher wouldn't even stop them. She just looked at the children and kept working with the smart kids. It felt like they didn't want me there."

It sounded like I had been in the same classroom with my brother. His face revealed the anxiety I felt mixed with a little fear at the thought of having to return the following day. A recurring and haunting thought that kept creeping into my mind was the vision of Mrs. Bauer walking up to me and asking me to recite the ABCs. Que loca (she was crazy). She didn't even realize that I had no idea what the ABCs were, let alone be able to recite them from beginning to end. In fact, the more I thought of what she had done to me and how she had embarrassed me in front of everyone, the greater my anger inside of me grew.

It was during the recess period that I began to learn the lessons of cruelty as practiced by children. Those Anglo kids had a meanness that seemed to always make me cry but only in the privacy of my home while I lay in my bed. I refused to show my weakness to the other kids, and I didn't want my father to know that I was having difficulty in school. It was so important to him for us to be successful. He always reminded us that education would be our way out of poverty.

After a while, there was less and less trouble in the schoolyard, but the difficulty in the classroom continued with Mrs. Bauer. She kept pushing me to recite the ABCs and expected me to use English in the same way they spoke it. She could not understand that some words were just difficult for me to pronounce, words like kitchen, chicken, chair, or chimney. Why was Mrs. Bauer so convinced that I could speak English like she could and pronounce those words like I even knew what they meant? The days went on, and I could sense the dissatisfaction in Mrs. Bauer's voice and tone toward me. I disappointed her. I felt as if I had done something wrong, but I didn't know what.

Finally, one day just like any other, a schoolteacher I had not seen before entered Mrs. Bauer's class. As I watched them greet each other, I noticed they were looking at me. Mrs. Bauer pointed in my direction, and I got the feeling that my world was about to change again without notice and without any of my say-so. I felt the same kind of fear that had enveloped my body one time when Immigration raided our home looking for people they called "wetbacks." That was a fear that would never go away. It would only hide until moments like this, when White people got together to plan things that would have a direct impact on me.

The discussion went on for quite some time until, finally, the new teacher came walking toward me with a look of determination. She had something in mind for me, and it was unclear what was coming. Standing in front of my desk, she said, "Hello, my name is Mrs. Brewster." Her greeting had little meaning to me because I felt an immediate threat and was not sure that I would stick around to get to know Mrs. Brewster. Little did Mrs. Brewster know that I distrusted her and would run if I had a chance. And if my father would allow it, I wouldn't return to school ever again. How could I know at that time that Mrs. Brewster would be my other teacher for the next couple of years?

Later, I came to understand what happened when the decision was made that I would attend two classes in different classrooms each day, something no other kid had to do—or at least that's what I thought. It seemed as if I was being picked on. At first, it wasn't clear what was going on or why I was being asked to go to another classroom. My first thought was that it was punishment for my escapades during recess and all those schoolyard fights. They must have realized that I really hated fighting. At least, I thought that they should know that I hated fighting. If it were up to me, making friends and playing with the kids would be my first choice. After all, this was the only place where kids made fun of me.

On that first morning in my new class, I noticed that there were only two other children in a tiny little room surrounded by windows that other kids would stare into as they walked by. There was barely enough room for four chairs and a single table. We were put on display for some unknown reason. Everyone could walk by and see the little flash cards we were using that had pictures of animals and people as if we couldn't distinguish what they were. I had no idea what the two other kids had done to get the same punishment. They didn't look very tough; maybe they just mouthed off or said some sort of cuss word. Who knew, and it really didn't matter.

It would be many years later that I learned that the special class was for what educators called "monos" and that the other two children in the same classroom were learning disabled.

Now I would not only carry the label of spic, greaser, and chief, but I would now be called dummy because I was being sent to the class that kids called the dummy class. It was hard to understand why they felt this way. I didn't feel dumb, and actually, I felt very smart. It was difficult for me to pronounce those difficult English words, but I was learning extremely fast. After all, I was expected to speak two languages. At seven, I spoke Spanish at home in the evenings, on the weekends, and every day after school. Then during the week in the classroom, I was expected to use English. For some reason, which seemed difficult, and it was especially stressful to speak English without an accent, which is something that I could tell disturbed Mrs. Bauer tremendously.

It seemed as if an accent was offensive to her and other teachers. They had little tolerance for anyone who did not speak the way they did. Later, I would learn that they thought I had a speech impediment and was learning disabled. My brother who was one year older, was in speech therapy as well, but we were in different classes so we would not speak Spanish at school. We traveled across the country so much that my brother started school a year late, and we ended up in the same grade.

Now on top of fighting those children who continually made fun of me, I was faced with the shame of having to attend special education classes for kids having a challenging time learning how to read. All I could think about was the shame it would bring my father if he knew I was going to the dummy class. He had such high hopes for me. The one bright spot was that I became friends with my fellow special needs classmates.

My time in the special class was spent pronouncing words and repeating sounds that challenged the configuration of my tongue. If you really stop and think about it, some of the English words were not meant to be pronounced by human beings. Mrs. Brewster turned out to be a truly kind person and seemed to understand that I had greater needs than could be provided by them or anyone in the school, and I think she could see that I was a dreamer. Her kindness, however, could not correct the damage that had been done by labeling me as a child with learning problems, a label that would follow me from grade school to middle school and eventually to high school.

This early label could have prevented me from eventually going to the university if I let it, but I've always been a dreamer, and I was determined to go to college regardless of what any teacher believed I could accomplish. They did manage to teach the accent out of my speech, and I now have a neutral speech pattern. Isn't education wonderful?

Our first three years in the Anglo schools did not get any easier. The children got more sophisticated in figuring out how to make fun of us and humiliate both my brother and me during recess as we tried to play with each other and ignore the meanness of this new world. Gerardo was on the other side of the building, but we found each other and were determined to give each other support.

They would have to come eventually. On one frigid winter day in the schoolyard, I had had enough and decided to use my skill in fighting to get back at those kids who refused to leave me alone. Fighting back became the only answer, and I was good at it. It was easy to resort to violence against anyone who made fun of me or anyone else who had a weakness. I became someone who would fight over any little thing and someone who would jump into a fight to protect other kids who would not fight for themselves. It was so easy to kick their ass that I never realized that I could control the activity in the playground with just a threat of violence. As time went on, fighting became the easiest answer to any controversy in the schoolyard.

Gerardo was not so eager to fight. He was more tolerant and had a degree of patience that served him well. I always admired him for his ability to remain calm during times of confrontation that would just make me angry and light a fire under my ass that was not easily extinguished. As I got more effective in my playground fighting skills, the kids began to leave me alone and play with me out of fear of getting their ass kicked. I was not offended by the fact that the other children would only play with me out of fear. Now, however, I've come to realize the damage I caused myself in choosing the way of violence. It caused me to become contrary to my upbringing and opposition to my spiritual well-being.

My early experience in public schools provided some valuable lessons on the struggles of people who have difficulty fitting in with mainstream society. I learned early that some children could not defend themselves and that they were not necessarily protected by the teachers who were there to provide the children with support. Trouble did not disappear when the children became more tolerant of my existence because it seemed that if the kids weren't picking on me, they would always find someone else to pick on. It became my mission to stand up for the kids who needed help. I found that the intervention on behalf of those kids gave me two pleasures: the opportunity to punch kids that I disliked for a good reason (or, at least I made myself feel like it was okay), and I could feel a sense of justice in helping someone who must have felt all alone as I did during my early times in school.

There were never any rewards except the personal satisfaction of knowing that I refused to let a little bit of cruelty continue. Survival in the schoolyard was early preparation for surviving in real life. My early education not only taught me to defend myself but look out for those who did not have the resources that I did and could not speak out. That is why I have chosen a career in public service and advocacy. The only difference now is that I do not have to choose violence to stand up for people who have been left out of the political and economic mainstream. I still carry with me that passion to defend anyone getting picked on by the schoolyard bullies who pick on anyone who looks different. And I have the support of the law.

Grade school was not much different. I went from school to school but always returned to Sunset Elementary, located in a community that became a regular stop on our yearly migration from Texas to the Pacific Northwest. Returning to Sunset year-to-year allowed me to make friendships that have lasted all my life, and it continues to be a place that I visit as a reminder of why I need to continue my work for others in my community that need help.

Life's journey brings to any person a gift bag of experiences and situations that they are supposed to learn from. My induction into the Anglo school system not only provided me with an education but also early lessons on discrimination. I learned that to have a different skin color is like wearing a sign on your back that screams out call me names, hate me, and try to kick my ass if you can. I also learned how to fight back physically and mentally in a way that I had not known before, even with my early lessons in the labor camps. Most important of all, however, I learned that many people in our small sphere of influence do not fight back and need our help, not because they are weak but because they are peace lovers or just innocent human beings. I chose to be one of those who chose to fight.

***

As a young boy, I saw some of my friends attempt to become part of the mainstream community by denying their origins, language, and culture. I observed friends walk into a school building as Xavier and walk out at the end of the day, calling themselves Willie. In our family, my brother Gerardo went to school for the first time with his name intact and came back home with the nickname "Jerry." The assimilation of many young people began by changing their names, which in turn began to impact their identity and create cultural confusion.

Denied

I went to enroll in school.

I was denied.

My clothes were funny.

I spoke in class,

I was denied.

My speech was impaired.

I tried to read out of the books.

I was denied.

My English was broken, unacceptable.

I was denied.

I tried to be a part of the school.

I was denied.

I was different, born into a world of

Different clothes, speech. and color.

They denied me.

This New World is hard to understand.

Someone! Please tell me.

What is wrong with me?

What is wrong with the world I come from?

My clothes are old and ragged.

My speech has an accent.

My skin is brown.

I am still a HUMAN BEING.

Please don't deny me anymore.

I have never denied you!

Growing up, I observed that the harder someone tried to blend into the Anglo community, the more noticeable they became to both communities. But more obvious was the more they tried to assimilate, the greater their emotional struggles of reconciling became. The transformers, as I like to call them, became neutralized to the things that added quality to their everyday living, like a baptism and the party that follows the celebration of a new Catholic arriving in our world. By trying to become who we are not, we end up missing who we are. In most cases, we succeed in becoming confused and not recognizing the legacy left to us by our ancestors. In trying to transform, they neutralized themselves.

The importance of us temporarily occupying this earth is to learn as much as possible while on our journey and to learn how to use ourselves as vessels of knowledge in order to contribute toward the survival and success of La Raza, which meant that when the time came, I would become part of a world that would meld both worlds into one people, the new people that the old people referred to as Raza.

CHAPTER 12
Middle School

I have never denied my background or my culture. I have taught my child to embrace her Mexican heritage, to love my first language, Spanish, to learn about Mexican history, music, folk art, food, and even the Mexican candy I grew up with.
~ Salma Hayeck

During school breaks and summers, the ancestral stories continued as we worked odd jobs during the "off" seasons. The summer before I entered junior high, I learned that my father had gotten a job at the Umatilla Army Depot. I would be going to junior high in Oregon. As I lay on the cotton mattress in the Chief Camp, staring out the dust-covered window, visions of being surrounded by White kids in a sterile school began to put the fear of God into my heart. The Chief Camp was the labor camp for migrant farm workers in Mabton, Washington. We had been working the migrant circuit in the Sunnyside and Mabton area for the early strawberry harvest. The early strawberry harvest leads to the rest of the summer working in the mint, beet, and potato fields and the cherry harvest. The cherry harvest was my favorite of all. I could already taste the sweetness of those ruby red Bing cherries. My mouth watered at the thought of the red juices seeping from their skin, bleeding red lifeblood for the soul of the laborer.

I approached the "teen" years believing that it had become my responsibility to continue to seek the truth of why my people had to leave the ancient land—the hidden truth that has been so elusive to the people of Aztlán. My only other recourse was to drop out of school and surrender to the beast of apathy. It was the instinct to give up and settle for what I knew. I kept thinking that life would be so much easier if I didn't have to go to school with these White people who seemed to have nothing but hatred in their hearts.

There were so many simple dreams that I heard people talk about as they worked side by side in 100-degree-plus weather with suffocating humidity. As the dream began to take hold, I saw that people would not pray for help or ask others for help. Instead, they began to plan what it would take to achieve their dreams. We were not in the habit of asking others for anything to be given to us, and we were willing to work for everything that we hoped to accomplish. As for me, all I wanted was to be treated like a human being, with respect. I was determined to work my way out of the fields, settle in a community, own a home and a car, and truly belong to this American dream. I was never allowed to give up on this America because my father and uncles were true believers. God, how my father and his side of the family had strength and faith that their hard work would be rewarded. Eventually, that faith and strength was passed on to me and school, indeed, was the conduit out.

The Classroom

Plastic chairs, silent, still without spirit,

A fluorescent world.

People come, gathered, to a place of knowledge.

Looking through each other's eyes,

Searching for an unwritten book.

Speaking into the walls,

Speaking in lost tongues, communicating noise.

Twisted noses and stretched bodies.

A junkyard of energy!

Paper tears of knowledge chasing

Zombies eating chocolate-covered donuts.

I was completing grade school and establishing myself as someone who could not be picked on and someone who would not take any shit, and I graduated into junior high. I had developed a reputation that followed me as a kid who would kick your ass if you looked at me in the wrong way. Now, I was faced with thinking about going through the same thing all over again in this new place that combined two grade schools into one. This meant that there was another entire group of kids who did not know of my reputation I had worked so hard to establish. I was just getting used to being left alone. I never did like fighting in the first place. All I ever wanted to do was to get those kids to leave me alone. They never did, and it started all over again, but in middle school, it did not take as long to establish my presence.

But now I was afraid. Afraid to go to this new town and a school filled with people who hate us so much. *Dear God, could you please let me go to school in Eagle Pass? Eagle Pass, where we all come from and where I know most of the families and they know me. I don't want to go to a place where I won't know a soul. Tias Rico and Lupe have watched over me since I was a baby, and I have always had Tios Camote and Cone to go to for advice. Now I will only have my father, who would be at work all day.*

I couldn't imagine who would take care of my sister Ide, who had the spirit of a wild horse on an open plain, or my sister Leonor, who had felt abandoned and hated the world because she never knew our mother, Dora. Gerardo would look out for himself, and I would get stuck with the housework and cooking for all of us because my sisters were too young for any of that. Things did not look good from where I sat. No family, no friends, only people who hated Mexicans. Great! We should all be happy that my father got a permanent job so we can settle down where we have no one to go to if we are having problems. How would living across the country from our family help us have a better life?

A melancholy set in as I thought about leaving the life of traveling with my aunts and uncles through the beautiful land that I had become accustomed to. I grew up in those beet fields with the asparagus fields as a playground, and I could eat delicious red apples whenever my heart desired. How could life be better than that for a twelve-year-old? The demanding work it took to make the little money we got from our effort did not seem so terrible if it meant keeping the family from separating. It was like the stories I had heard about the prophecy of ancient lands and how families had been split apart to explore new worlds in search of the elusive truth. Exploring new worlds for what? I thought the entire world had already been explored and what exactly was this truth the old people talked about? They have always talked about finding that special place for our people called La Raza and that in this place, we would be treated with respect, and we would understand the truth of living on this earth.

The summer seemed as endless as it had always been, surrounded by the sweet smells of alfalfa, and engulfed by the buzzing of honeybees. Sometimes as we drove down the back country roads on the way to work in the early mornings. I would catch the scent of Wrigley's chewing gum. It took some time to realize it was mint fields. Toppenish farmers were known for growing mint with a bittersweet taste in the leaves.

Once the signals of fall began to show themselves, we began to have more pleasant working days but less daylight, which meant we had to get up earlier to get out into the fields and put in a full day. One of the first signs of the change in the season was the decrease in humidity; that damp, soaking feeling through my blue jeans and sticking to my skinny legs began to disappear. The closer to fall and the further away from summer meant that my time would soon come to leave the only family I had known to join my father in Hermiston.

The people in this new place would know nothing of who I was, where I was coming from, and what I saw through these eyes that had been claimed by ancient souls. My spirit is one that must roam free like a wild parrot in the Yucatan jungle. Since my birth, my family had not tried to control my wild spirit or my sense of exploration; my family was mostly there to guide my freedom. In the eyes of my aunts, I could do no wrong and they would constantly reinforce how smart I was. Now I was faced with managing what I would say or think for fear that the people in this new place would not understand what was in my heart and not accept my freedom of thought. Fear was chewing at my heels. Fear of not fitting in, of not knowing what to do or not knowing how to speak English well enough to be accepted.

Walking through the front door of that three-story sandstone building was a frightening moment. Being twelve years old provides a person with a lot of courage to explore many different worlds without fear, but only those that are fun. From the outside, the building looked like it was forbidden. As I walked through the huge double doors with my father, it seemed as if the doors were twenty feet tall, and the sun was swallowed up by the density of the sandstone skeleton of the building. The shadows of fluorescent lighting surrounded all the children. The purity of the fresh air was snuffed out by the stench of the chemicals from those lights inside Armand Larve Junior High School. Who the hell was Armand Larve anyway?

Walking toward me was a huge White man. Oh no! I hoped he wouldn't stop and talk to me. But when you try to avoid someone, they are usually the ones most interested in talking to you. His eyes caught mine and he stopped and leaned forward as if he were bending over and introduced himself. As he reached for my hand to shake it, I saw that his hands were huge. His thumbnail was bigger than my whole thumb combined.

"Hello, my name is Mr. Williams," he said as he crushed my hand. I could barely understand his thick accent. I later learned he was from somewhere in the South, I recall someone saying he was from Alabama. He had more of a drawl than any Texan I'd ever heard.

Staring into the empty eyes of the children walking past me up and down the dark hallways, I could hear some laughter and playing but nothing that sounded like the wild spirit of the camp kids. These kids seemed controlled in their behavior and their eyes did not wander. How could I get any of their attention long enough to make a friend? My world was caving in on me. It felt as if the freedom I'd had up to this point was about to change. I couldn't imagine what would make the Anglo kids laugh. How could I joke around with them if I didn't have any understanding of their humor?

Finally, as the conversation with Mr. Williams and my father was ending, I spotted three kids about my age who looked like me with black hair and brown skin. Just as I spotted them, they quickly walked around the corner and disappeared. I hoped that I would get a chance to meet them later. I wondered if they came from Eagle Pass or someplace nearby like Carrizo Springs or Quemado.

I overheard my father telling Mr. Williams to let him know if he had any problem with me. But I knew he was not going to have any problem with me because I wouldn't be going to school if I could get away with it. My plans were to leave as quickly as I arrived. With goodbyes out of the way, Mr. Williams asked me to follow him and said he was going to introduce me to my homeroom teacher, whatever that was. This marked the beginning of a colorful career as a student with a lot of talent but known as a student who didn't apply himself.

It was a couple of weeks before I met the other Brown kids. First, I met Robert Hernandez wandering through the hall, off on the far side of the building, where he was either delaying going to class or getting ready to launch the great escape. I yelled out to him and motioned for him to come toward me. As we walked toward each other, another guy showed up, coming toward us from the other hall. We met at the intersection of the main hall that connected to the wing that would become our hangout; it had an exit out at the back of the building onto Route 1. I stood silent as Robert said hello to his buddy. When they looked toward me, it was as if they were waiting for a great statement.

All I could think of to say was, "My name is Victor, and I am Raza." Robert looked at me and said, "Hey man, what is Raza?"

I knew then they were not from my part of the country. As I stood frozen, the other kid broke the silence and said, "I'm an Oglala Sioux. I'm from Pine Ridge, South Dakota. My name is Ben, but people call me Benny."

We talked for hours during those few minutes between the bells. As the ringing began, we agreed to meet at the same place right after the last class to plan our first adventure. That was the beginning of friendships that would sustain our lives and prove to be a bond that would hold in its firmness beyond this life.

The afternoon finally came, and it was time to meet my new friends. Well, they weren't quite friends yet, but at least they were new people to hang out with. I rushed to the designated meeting place; I didn't notice anyone along the way until a huge arm reached out and grabbed me, pulling me back in my tracks. It was Mr. Williams who bellowed, "Where are you going so fast, young man?" He looked into my eyes and said, "No one runs in my hallway. Do we understand each other?"

"Si," was all I could say for fear of getting punished.

I finally made it to the agreed-upon rendezvous with Robert, Ben, and a beautiful young girl who looked like one of the

Mexican girls from the work camps who went to the weekend dances. Robert smiled when he caught me focused on this young beauty and said, "This is my sister Susan."

Susan, I thought to myself. Robert and Susan …these are not Mexican names. Why would any Raza family give their children Anglo names? The schools had changed their names, like my brother Gerardo, whose name was changed the first time he went to an Anglo school. Now that I stop to think about it, there weren't many children who attended Anglo schools who didn't come back with different names. But it really didn't matter because I was making new friends and that was all that was important at the moment. Susan was quiet and listened to our nonsense as we decided to walk to Robert's house to discuss our next plan of action.

From that first meeting, we became closer friends than I had imagined. We would meet after classes and at the end of the day to plan and execute the escapades of young boys trying to be men. As we got older, our adventures went from pranks like setting stop signs on fire to throwing rocks at semi-trailers as they sped past us on route one. Those were more serious activities that could eventually bring trouble to our doorsteps. Our courage was beyond reason, and our judgement was not even present. We went from juvenile behavior to waiting for drunken old men stumbling out of the local hot spot so drunk that they couldn't talk, and we asked them to buy us beer. If they refused, we threatened to beat it out of them.

Getting beer for the weekend dances was always the challenge until we started to get to know some of the older guys in town. The older crowd we began hanging out with were the ones people called "greasers" or "hoods." Some of the guys had already been in prison for drugs or theft. Prison didn't matter much if your opportunity to make friends was limited to begin with. We possessed a certain sense of invincibility and naiveté when it came to the company we kept and our ability to avoid law enforcement.

As in most small rural towns, weekend activities typically ended with parties along the river, in a park, or in the mountains that were only two hours away. Of course, there would be drinking if we could find someone to buy us beer. We could always find someone who felt sorry for us and convince them to buy us a case of our favorites: Schlitz malt liquor and Coors. Coors was almost impossible to get because it wasn't sold in Oregon. Beer was a necessity for the weekend dances. It would have been criminal to go to the weekend dance at the civic recreation center without being a bit on the tipsy side. Drinking, driving, and fighting—a deadly recipe for catastrophe—were all a part of the rituals that we practiced every weekend to accommodate our rite of passage into manhood. Going to a dance sober was unthinkable, and to leave the dance without getting into a fight was unheard of. We always had an enemy waiting for us with revenge on their mind for some past action, nipping at our heels, demanding satisfaction. Of course, it was important that you win the fight and that someone witnessed the feat.

The adrenaline of dancing, the tribal dances of love and war worked us into a frenzy and prepared us for the fights that followed immediately after the dance. This was at a site away from town so the cops could not show up and stop the fight or, worse yet, throw someone in jail. Cars showed up as people arrived to watch the gladiators exhibit their ability in the ring formed by the cars forming a circle. The car headlights served as the lighting for the gladiator's arena. Once the ring was formed, everyone would pull out their beer and begin to drink, waiting for the warriors to appear. It would usually take a while to get there because of the extra beer or whisky needed to drink ourselves into a readiness state to face the ring surrounded by people you would see the next morning working in grocery stores, gas stations, or the county library.

You had to be the winner. There was no way you could lose and show your face in town again. I had to face that ring many times not because I considered myself a fighter or enjoyed fighting but because people wanted to prove themselves by fighting me. I never considered myself a warrior and always wanted to be left alone in peace. Initially, I faced the ring to prove my manhood, but eventually, I was forced to face the ring with those who had something to prove by kicking the shit out of me. No one ever kicked my ass. What these young men did not know was that I had been in training for this kind of fighting since I was nine. I had no qualms about using a tire iron, beer bottle, two-by-four, or anything that would provide me with an equalizer if the opponent was bigger than me. The early lessons I received from my uncles and men in the labor camp was that there was no such thing as fair fighting. There was only one outcome that I wanted in a fight, and that was to win, no matter the strategy.

I still don't know why I fought so much. I have always deplored violence, but it seemed as if others were always testing me. If I were left alone to follow my own path, I would never have chosen violence as one of my tools. At one time, before I discovered girls at the age of twelve, I wanted to be a priest. My interests were to live in peace and just laugh, joke, and love. I would never have entered the ring if it were not a requirement for survival.

The fights usually ended the same. A victor rose from the powdery soil, with a thin coat of dust covering his body like talcum powder on a baby. Spectators watched the dark shadows as they danced back and forth, landing blows and then dancing away until the pugilist would leap from his victim with a smile, broadcasting their accomplishment. The blood begins to show itself through the dust as it is absorbed and caked on the victor's face. The winner strutted around the circle in a victory lap. The loser moaned from the pain of defeat and the reality of the damage from a broken nose, an ear bitten loose, or both eyes swollen shut from damage inflicted by cowboy boots and fists.

Drinking and fighting were not the main reasons to go to the

Saturday night dance. It was about the only time we could enjoy getting close to any of the Anglo girls. Dating Anglo girls was forbidden fruit for Mexican and Indian kids like Robert, Ben, and me. When we did have an Anglo girlfriend, it was hidden from our parents and any other family that would have objections. It was especially difficult when the girls had brothers older than we were. That usually meant that we would have to fight them. Fighting to have an Anglo girlfriend was common, and there were no Latina girls to date except for Robert's sister, Susan, but she was Robert's sister and always left alone. While we were treating her with so much respect, she ended up dating an Anglo boy that none of us trusted or even liked. We ended up giving him a nickname, Boner, for many varied reasons, including the one that you can imagine.

Romance was not in our realm of expertise. We never quite fit the role of Latin lovers even though I always had the impression that the girl's parents never trusted us because of that stereotype. Admittedly, we were fortunate to always have the kindest and most beautiful girlfriends. With that kind of good luck, I never recognized the difference in how we were raised. Where I came from, and the language I spoke could make the difference in whether romance could sustain a lifetime. Being a Mexican seemed to eventually come up and make a difference as to whether we could love forever or not. Meeting girls at the dances was the easy part of life; even getting them to leave with us to go do a little more drinking was easy. The hard part was maintaining a long-term relationship like the other kids who always had the same girlfriend throughout junior high or high school. Usually, we all ended up with another drinking partner, and our evening would continue beyond its original intent.

Not much time had passed since the first time the threesome had met, that I began to realize that my innocence had slipped away. Drinking, fighting, cursing, and chasing girls was not the way I had been raised but it was quickly turning into a daily occurrence. In a slow turn of events, our small group of three had grown to five as we had befriended two Anglo kids: a huge cowboy named Bill Ellis and a kid with some Gypsy blood in him named John Bartley. Like us, they were different from the rest of the kids at school. Bill stood six feet five inches and weighed about 230 pounds. He was always loud and physical. Even when he played around, he could hurt you while having fun. John was quiet and a thinker who was always reading some book. I remember thinking that he was a genius, the smartest guy we ran around with and the smartest person I have ever known. When John laughed or saw something funny, he sneered and then start panting like he was thirsty. He always carried this sneer, as if he knew something that no one else knew, and he had an infectious laugh that could draw you into laughter even if you did not know what was so funny.

The group had formed, and the bond was made. Our lives would be forever tied to each other through the youth we shared. We would also grow closer by revealing our inner weaknesses to each other as we experienced passion through fear and violence, growing into manhood. Fate brought five young men together so we could learn from each other, love, understand life, and support each other. While we did not accumulate the wisdom growing up, on reflection, it is clear to the two of us who are left that it was a plan from God that we meet and shape our destinies together.

As we grew older and matured, we became more subtle in our behavior and more considerate and respectful with girls. We lost the taste for beer and began to explore the different effects of whiskey, marijuana, and other drugs that would give us a rush and allow us to escape our ghosts. We were interested in pursuing the rush of danger, feeling the unknown, and the anxiety of losing control. Just as we thought that there was no future for us in the Anglo world as Brown people, we had united with buddies who possessed a loyalty like what we had grown up with. Without each other, we were loners. Even if we were only a small group, it was like a family. We cared for each other, and we treated each other with respect and unconditional loyalty. Our buddies didn't get that at home. They knew they could always count on us. We would always be there for each other.

After graduation from beer to whiskey and from junior high school to high school, we began smoking dope. This was not a fad at the time. It was looked down upon and we had to keep it hidden as it wasn't something our other friends at school were doing. Our exposure to drugs came from the friends we made who had been recently released from prison. There were always a few guys we would meet who were either right out of prison or had been in prison. Most of the guys we hung out with had all been in reform school or were on their way there except Robert, Ben, and me.

I had spent most of my life traveling with my family and working in the fields. Robert had done the same kind of work in the Midwest, mostly in Nebraska, and Ben came from the reservation. We all had some early protection provided by a close family that changed when we moved to an all-White community away from the rest of our extended family.

I no longer had my aunts and uncles to go to when my father wasn't around. I had to face the newfound freedom on my own without help, knowing how to manage this freedom to go anywhere and do anything I wanted. My father was always working, and my only responsibility was to make sure that my sisters, Ide, and Leonor, had clean clothes and something to eat.

My friend Ben had six siblings and a mother who was truly kind, a nurse at the local hospital. His father was unemployed, a World War II veteran fighting the ghosts that he brought back from the war in the Pacific and used alcohol as his weapon to fight the ghosts, unlike my father, who chose to fight his ghosts from the war with a permanent silent meditation. Bill's father was constantly beating him as punishment, trying to get him to stop beating up everyone else. Every time Bill's dad beat him, Bill went to school and took it out on someone else. It did not matter who. Sometimes when we got drunk, he would even try to fight with us, but we would all kick his ass until he couldn't move.

Then there was Robert, whose father criticized everything he did; nothing Robert ever did was good enough. Robert's father constantly yelled that he was a 'Goddamn cruddy kid, a good-for-nothing." We heard his mantra so often that we would mock each other by calling ourselves "Goddamn cruddy kids" to ease some of Robert's pain. We all had some baggage that we refused to unpack and kept wearing around our necks. We were constantly fighting to get rid of our baggage with no understanding of how to do that.

CHAPTER 13
High School

Because of him/her my face becomes wide.
(This was said when someone's child – a boy – or girl or else someone's pupil, was well – taught, well - brought up.)
~ Mexica

While I spent most of my free time with my friends, I still had family duties that I would never have considered neglecting. My brother Gerardo had always been distant from the rest of us. I think this was because so much of his formative years were spent in Mexico with our grandparents and relatives while the rest of us traveled with the caravans to the camps. Gerardo had not experienced the hatred and disgust launched toward Mexicans displayed by all those small rural towns across the West. He had been protected and had a different attitude about living in this new place.

Sometimes I wished that I could have been more like him. It always seemed as if he fit into the White world and that everyone had accepted him into the main circles of activity. He would get invited to parties that my friends and I would never see. Of course, my view and my buddies' view of fun were much different than the socialites or "socies" as we called them. Our idea of fun was alcohol, drugs, and driving around and eventually ending up in trouble. Our anger at being left out was displayed through many of our evening activities that, often, bordered on the illegal. Graffiti became my trademark.

I had a hidden talent for art that surfaced in spray-painted symbols of defiance wherever I could find a strategically placed wall. The word was out through our network that I was the king of outdoor art. My passion was cultivated by a teacher who could see through my anger and recognize my creative spirit. Mrs. Hansen believed in me so much that she supplied me with oil paints and brushes, which I could never have afforded. During my time in her class, she gave me one-on-one instruction, wisely disguising her counseling attempts, which were all about my potential.

My interest in art grew to become such a driving force that I would dream about my next painting. I began a mural on my bedroom wall and only worked on it late at night so my father wouldn't know that I was painting a cityscape in my bedroom. The secret artwork only lasted about a month, and I had almost finished the painting when my father found out. Of course, I was punished, and it was the most brutal of all punishments: he went for almost two weeks without talking to me. He did not say one thing one way or another. All I knew was that he was pissed and that I had better cover that painting up. I did not realize that because I had painted the mural with oils, the painting would show through every time I tried painting over it with latex paint. After several coats of latex, we had to wallpaper the room to hide my work. What a depressing day that was, that day that I had to cover up all the late-night work I had done, to be hidden forever.

While art was my talent, my friends had other talents that were never discovered by teachers or parents. Robert had always been a scholar, constantly with a book in his hand. Robert could make any plant grow and grew the most fantastic pot plants I ever saw. I was the dreamer with art chasing my soul. Talent was not what people saw when they looked into our eyes, though. They saw a spic, a greaser, an Indian, and poor. God, what a waste of bright minds! What could have been accomplished if we had been discovered all those years ago?

Thank God for one kind woman who knew how to help me channel my anger from the deepest part of my heart and soul. She had the wisdom to understand that something was fighting to get out. Mrs. Hansen caught me one day in the hall in the middle of a practical joke and asked me to sign up for her art class. "I hear that you're a good artist on the street and that you might be an excellent painter." Mrs. Hansen would become the angel who guided me off the streets and into the classroom. I didn't know what she was up to when we first met, but my path had already begun to change.

Our escapades continued all through high school. We couldn't do anything without getting into some kind of fight with someone. If they weren't after me, they would be after Robert. Ben was the peacekeeper; he never wanted to fight anyone. My rule was to get in the first blow, whether it was a punch, kick, or any kind of equalizer. Anger can provide an unpredictable life for a young person, and control is not in the formula.

Cruising the gut was a favorite pastime for anyone with a license and a vehicle. In our group, Robert and I were the drivers. I drove a 1949 green Chevy pick-up with a custom cab, and Robert had a 1948 flat-head V-8 Ford pick-up, both in excellent condition. We went through at least three tanks of gas a week cruising from one end of town to the other, looking for action, mostly looking to pick up the girls. After all, that's what we were all about. Occasionally, we'd get lucky and pick someone up and go to the park for a couple of hours out in the desert in the middle of sagebrush and tumbleweed. We weren't after love, just the excitement of exploring sex. Rarely did any long-term relationships flourish from an evening of cruising the gut and parking out in the sticks.

On one of those occasions, instead of driving way out of town I chose to park at the gravel pit just three miles out. This turned out to be a serious mistake. It was the first time that I went to the park with someone that I genuinely cared about. It never crossed my mind that some of my buddies might be cruising around at the same time. The worst of all scenarios developed and cured me forever from having sex in a vehicle out in the countryside where I couldn't see anyone coming.

I was out with my one and only real high school sweetheart, Linda, whom I would protect to the death and most certainly if her honor were in question. Just as we had taken our clothes off and we were lying with each other, totally naked, when suddenly car lights jumped through the back windshield and blinded both of us for an instant. Shock and fear choked every sound from my mouth as Linda began to scream, quickly sitting up and trying to find her clothes. All I could think of was trying to start the pick-up and get the hell out of there.

It seemed like hours to start my truck, and finally the engine ignited. I punched the gas pedal, spinning out as I spit gravel at the car that began to follow us. Only one thought was going through my mind: getting away from that car behind us. I wanted to keep the guys from finding out that Linda had been with me. Her honor was particularly important in a small town like Hermiston, where everyone would know what had happened by the time they were sipping their morning coffee.

As I spun out, another car was coming directly toward us, and I yelled to Linda to get on the floorboard so no one could spot her. There she was, screaming, crouching naked, and hoping that they wouldn't catch up with us. I took off across the desert, looking for the most impassable roads because I was driving a pick-up, and the other vehicles were cars. My foolish thinking led me to believe that they wouldn't follow me down some of those tough roads. The chase lasted for about forty-five minutes through the most difficult terrain in eastern Oregon until, finally, the headlights began to get more distant, although they were still coming.

During the chase, Linda had time to get dressed, but I was still naked and now driving into town looking for a place to pull over and hide so I could dress. Finally, I spotted a place: the bowling alley had a dark side of its parking lot directly behind the kitchen. I pulled in, and our honor was saved, and no one was the wiser. They could only guess who had been with me, and I never told anyone, not even Robert or Ben.

As buddies and partners, we always managed to have a great time, no matter what obstacle. Romance was always on the front burner for all of us, and sometimes we ended up with a girlfriend. Robert was the one who took romance and love much too seriously and seemed to fall in love more often than anyone else. For him, every relationship was always his only love. His pain still haunts him from the loss of love that he felt he could never reach.

What Robert could never understand is that it was never intended for us to settle down with those young, pretty, blue-eyed White girls. They were always out of bounds, and their parents only tolerated our dating them with the hopes that it would blow over. My fortune with my youthful romances transformed into more than just teenagers thinking we were in love. I have remained in contact with some of my earliest girlfriends from as far back as the third grade. What we thought was love has become genuine friendships that have allowed us to stay in touch and share each other's lives as we grew into adulthood and experienced all the good and bad of life.

As for my friends, Ben loved everyone, and Bill has only loved one girl as long as I have known him. None of us were particularly good at understanding love. I can only think that we did not receive guidance or didn't have the opportunity to observe role models who could guide us on how to share and receive love. I think it is because we all came from unstable families.

One of the last big parties came in my senior year. The party culminated with about thirty of us having to appear in court for destroying a farmer's house. Almost everyone on the football team was involved, including some of the kids from the wealthiest families, which I believe kept us out of jail. It began innocently, just a discussion about having a party to celebrate our last football game as seniors. Everyone seemed to agree that a party would top off a great season.

Ben and I played football together from junior high to that final game in high school. Being involved in athletics taught us some responsibility and the idea that we needed other people to be successful. In small towns, athletics can sometimes keep young people from getting into trouble with the police, especially if you're a good athlete and on the varsity team. I think it was a saving grace for both Ben and me on a couple of occasions, including the incident at the farmhouse that brought both the socies and the greasers to the same courtroom.

Our party idea had only two problems: a place to have the kegger and where to get the keg. We had never been accused of being geniuses, so our solution shouldn't have surprised anyone. I can't remember who first brought it up, but one of us in the group blurted out that we could cruise the country roads until we found a farmhouse that looked like the family was out or on vacation. We all knew that once the harvest was completed, the likelihood of a farmer being on vacation was extremely high.

Finding a place, however, was difficult by just cruising the country roads, and it did not produce results. Finally, Bill said he knew someone who would be gone for five days, and we could use that house. We went out that evening to scope it out. The house was located about eight miles out of town on a country road that offered a vantage point as we would be able to see any vehicles coming down the road. The only drawback was that it was located on a dead-end lane down a long single-lane driveway that would allow only one car at a time in or out. The house was empty, and we were ready for a party except for figuring out how we would get the beer.

Buying the beer turned out to be easier than we expected. We approached one of the rich kids we knew worked at his dad's grocery store and knew he had the key. What an opportunity! We only had to convince Dennis that he should bring the beer. Dennis, for some reason, decided to listen to us, even though he knew we had always been in trouble. Mission accomplished. Immediately after the game, we met in the parking lot of the school, drove to the store, loaded up the beer, and headed to the farmhouse to start the party.

The party had been in the planning stage for such a long time, and the fact that the greasers and the socies would be going to this momentous event turned it into a party bigger than any of us had ever imagined. The cars began to arrive as quickly as we had. Before we knew it, every room of the three-bedroom house was packed like sardines with screaming seniors, drinking beer, and acting out. For many of the kids, it was their first-time drinking beer and smoking a little pot. Not everyone was comfortable with the pot, but everyone got into the beer and whiskey we had pulled together.

After three hours of partying, things seemed to be under control, with few disputes and small outbreaks between sweethearts arguing about who loved who the most and who cared or who didn't. Some guys were posturing like young bulls, challenging anything that appeared threatening, especially if they thought they caught someone eyeing or making a move on their girlfriend. Incidents became much more sensitive if one of the greasers was flirting or even making some headway with one of the rich girls.

Around midnight and in predictable fashion, little skirmishes began to break out. Tempers began to percolate, bubble, and boil. You could feel the friction between two groups that had been brought together that typically were not exposed to each other. Here they had to share the same space. It almost seemed as if there were opposing values from kids who lived in the same town. I knew that there would be trouble. I had felt and seen those looks before. My survival skills had been hone so much that I was sensitive to nonverbal messages, those signals people send when you've violated their space. It felt as if an eruption was imminent. The only missing ingredient was someone pulling the trigger to launch a major blow-up.

Suddenly, from one of the back bedrooms, kids were popping out of the screens and jumping through the windows. There was panic everywhere, and I couldn't figure out why until I saw the red flashing light coming down that long stretch of country road. It was the cops. I leaped into the air like a gazelle escaping a predator and raced toward the back door only to run into a traffic jam of bodies shoving each other to get out. People were running in all directions into the field to hide from the cops. I saw one guy running through the backyard and disappearing into the earth. He ran over an old storm cellar that had given way to age and swallowed him into its tomb. As I approached the cellar, I heard groaning echoes from the moss-ridden stone walls. It was Robert. He yelled out, "Where's Bennie?"

I spotted Ben getting up from the ground as he dusted himself off. I heard a loud "Shit!" coming from Ben.

"What happened, man?" I yelled and Ben yelled back, "The asshole ran over me trying to get away from the cops."

After stumbling around for about twenty minutes, we finally got together enough to spot the car with the red flashing light pulling up the dirt driveway and realized it wasn't a cop. It was a carload of guys who had graduated the year before who were trying to disrupt the party. When they finally reached the house, chaos immediately broke out again as the driver was yanked from the car and someone began beating him. Major fighting broke out throughout the house, and people started to get more violent as panic set in. I saw one guy kicking and punching the water heater as if were an enemy soldier in hand-to-hand combat, pulling and yanking at it until he ripped it from the wall. Water began to spew out. Walls were being kicked in, the front door had been torn from its hinges, and every window in the house had been broken out.

When the party was finally over and everyone had gone, we

were left with the guilt of what had happened to the farmer's home. I had no idea how I would make things right. It was never our intention to cause this kind of harm to the family that lived in this house. Now it was too late to turn back and there was no way to correct the damage. The party of the year had turned into total destruction. Driving away from the site, I got a sinking feeling that the story of this party was not over.

Several weeks passed before the police showed up at the school asking questions. They had a list of names and kids they were going to talk to. One by one, I watched them go into the principal's office, wondering if these rich kids knew the code and that they were bound to silence even at the cost of taking the entire blame themselves. For some reason, I could imagine that one of those rich kids would spill their guts. That is exactly what happened! Everyone at the kegger was named and served with papers to appear in county court.

The only thing that saved us from going to jail is that both the rich and poor kids alike were guilty of the same crime. Of the thirty who had to go to court, most were richer than the three of us. The judge decided that we were all guilty and that we would have to pay for materials and repairs to the house. Luckily, one of the kids had a father who owned the local lumber company, and another father had a construction company. They agreed to provide the materials for the repairs, and we had to agree to do the work.

I had to work for the rest of the year to pay for my share. I was glad to do it because it kept me from going to jail, but most of all it helped me get rid of the guilt I had to carry for being involved in planning a party that caused so much damage to the home of a hard-working family. Even though I did not cause the damage, it would never have happened if I had not helped with the planning.

Times were sometimes difficult growing up in a foreign culture away from the roots of my soul and the people who carried the story of our birth as a people. I missed the stories of the ancient ancestors and their travels, the beauty of Aztlán and the journey that we were all involved with, even if sometimes we forgot what it was that we were to accomplish. God, how I missed the language, music, the smell of the food cooking on an outdoor stove, and the laughter that came from struggle. I missed the dances and the beautiful girls with shiny black hair that swished as they walked.

Memories were all I had while I lived and grew into adulthood in an all-Anglo world. Even the kindness of the young women who loved me did not wash away the pain of being transplanted into a world that could not replenish my lifeblood.

CHAPTER 14
Adulting

La vida te prepara para que seas capaz de crear tu propio final Feliz.
(Life prepares you to be able to create your own happy ending.)
~Dicho

It sems like yesterday that I would get up at four-thirty in the morning to get ready to go to work by five and rush back home to make sure my sisters were up, had breakfast, and were off to school. Working while in school was not a choice. It afforded me my school clothes, lunch money, and the basic needs of a teenager. I could only work enough hours to buy the basics; any additional time spent at work meant that I would have to neglect my responsibilities at home. While most of my friends saw me as a reckless teenager, wild and carefree, I had assumed responsibilities that typically belonged to an adult.

As my high school years ended, I observed that some of my friends seemed to think of nothing but having fun and making plans to go to college. On the weekends we would get together at a place we called Hat Rock that got its name because it resembled a Pilgrim's hat.

For as long as anyone could remember, weekend kegger parties on the sandy beach of the Columbia River at Hat Rock Park were a rite of passage. This tradition, older than our impending high school graduation, was a beloved fixture for generations. Graduating classes flocked to the park, drawn by its reputation as a haven, far from the prying eyes of local police. It was common knowledge among locals—a secret hiding in plain sight.

Looking back, I realize now that our belief in evading a police raid was naive. It never crossed my mind that everyone knew exactly where we were and what we were up to at Hat Rock. Yet, the charm of the place lay not just in its secluded location but also in its unspoken understanding: a tacit agreement between the community and the youth. The park, with its many nooks and crannies, provided a perfect place to crash overnight if someone had too much to drink. It was as if the landscape itself had conspired to keep us safe, allowing the tradition to continue uninterrupted year after year.

We built a huge campfire, told stories of our exploits, and drank beer from the large keg in Dixie cups, not minding how many we drank until it was too late. There was always someone who did not drink, and we looked out for each other, making sure we got home.

That summer of 1968 was the first time I realized that the next period in my life would be yet another stage and that I would have to uproot once more to experience things I had not thought of or seen before. This new phase would be another time of learning and accumulating more understanding of how my past knowledge and what I was about to learn "fit" with the stories I heard as a boy of what our destiny would be. I had an overwhelming feeling that I wanted to go to college but had no idea how to get there. I knew my family did not have the money, and we had no clue how other families paid for college. If that were not enough, I knew that I had not excelled in school, mostly because working and helping my family was more important, which meant that there was no time to study.

Not being able to find the time to study was not enough of an excuse. Up to now, my biggest barrier was thinking in the moment and how to survive, and not in "making ready" for the future. How could I prepare myself for what my elders had told me over those campfires in my youth? My mission was to accumulate knowledge that provided a greater understanding of who I could become by understanding where I came from.

The lowest point of my early years after high school was one evening when I found myself walking alone on the football field, wondering where time had gone and what I had accomplished. I could not think of any major accomplishment other than surviving. As I walked and jogged around the track, I recalled many positive memories that were gone, and I was stuck not knowing what my next step would be. Tears began to fill my eyes, thinking that this might be the end of my explorations, that I would not learn anymore and never discover what it would take to fulfill what was expected of me or to arrive at my destiny.

The next morning, I went out to the Union Pacific railroad yard to look for a job. As luck would have it, an older man knew of me from playing on the football team. This opened the door for me to have a discussion with him that led to a job offer on the bridge crew painting railroad bridges. Mr. Williamson offered me a summer job on the road crew, and I accepted, not knowing what would be expected of me or if I could even do the job. After all, painting bridges sounded simple enough; how hard could it be to paint?

My first day began in a community sixty miles away, where I would live in a railroad car and go out with the crew to work on a bridge that spanned across a river. I arrived at the site, got out of my pickup, and started walking over toward the edge of the bridge where all the equipment had been set up. A man walked up to me and extended his hand. "My name is Jim. You must be the new guy."

Before I even said yes, he told me to grab an air pressure chisel, go to the top overhead beam of the bridge, and start chiseling out the black rusted pits to prepare the cross beam for a coat of primer. I looked up at the top of the bridge, not knowing how to even get up there, and said, "Hell no, you go up there and do that."

The supervisor stood quiet and calm and stared at me for a bit. Then he said, "You either go up there and do your job or go back to town."

It seemed like an eternity before I got the courage to walk over to the equipment, grabbed the chisel and walked toward the bridge. At the base, I started climbing up an inclined beam with the greatest caution and some hesitation until I reached the top. With a rope, I pulled up the chisel, got a firm grip, and began chiseling with my legs, straddling the cross beam like I was riding a horse. Wouldn't you know it? I no sooner got started than a torpedo went off. A torpedo is a small firecracker-like explosive clamped onto the track a mile up the track that makes a loud explosive sound to let everyone know that a train is coming. I did not have time to climb down. I could see it coming and had no idea what to expect.

As it got closer, the sound got louder, and the bridge began to vibrate, shake, and sway. Then, suddenly, the train was on the bridge, and it began to sway and shake even more. As the engine passed under me, I could feel the exhaust from the engines blowing up against my body. I held on for dear life, and it felt as if this would never end. When it was over, I knew I had been introduced to fear and understood what it could do.

My summer was spent working with the road crew, making union wages for the first time, and saving money to go to a community college twenty miles away from our home. It was all I could afford, and they would accept me with my average record and the golf score tally of my SAT test. If my efforts had been any worse, any type of college would have been out of the question, let alone some large university. It was a safe bet to accuse me of having a wild imagination. But instinctively, I had a sense that a college degree was something that I would achieve. It was the encounter with my childhood curandera that created this misplaced confidence in my abilities. by telling me that I would have a long, healthy life and would become famous.

The Naysayer

Can you imagine having the balls to go against the advice given to me by Mr. Wilson, my high school counselor? It still makes me angry to think that he could have prevented me from fulfilling my dream. Mr. Wilson had called me in for a brief discussion on what I would be doing after graduation. This was my opportunity to talk about my dreams and aspirations.

Mr. Wilson was a small slender man with a crew cut and white walls around his ears who looked as if he was a drill sergeant in the military. His hair was so blonde it was almost white, and he always looked angry. My only knowledge of him was from football because he was the assistant coach for the backfield. Mr. Wilson did not seem like the kind of person you would go to if you needed help or advice. I didn't know who set up the meeting and assumed that everyone would be meeting with the counselors. Walking into the principal's office gave me a sinking feeling, and I felt short of breath. It was as if I had been called in for punishment.

Sitting in his waiting room forced me to focus on my purpose for being there and to ask myself what my goals in life were. A buzzer sounded on the telephone, and I could hear Mr. Wilson's voice over the intercom. "Please have Victor come in." I was pointed down a hall and to the left.

Knocking on Mr. Wilson's door, I could hear that he was on the phone, talking about how great of a student Doug Walters was and that he would be successful at the university. I knocked again, feeling nervous as hell. With the coldness of a bitter winter wind, his voice shot out, "Come in."

Instinct told me that this meeting was not going to go well as soon as Mr. Wilson's eyes glared into mine. "What are your plans after graduation?"

My response, of course, was as honest as possible because it was the first that popped into my mind. "Go to college and study to be an art teacher."

Silence filled the room, and Mr. Wilson sat motionless and without expression. Finally, the silence broke when he reached over to a file and opened it. "Victor," he said, in a slow deliberate voice, "it would be better if you thought of going to a vocational school and studying to become a mechanic or some type of technician. From what your file shows, you could not succeed in a university. Your grades seem to show that you wouldn't be able to make it."

I remember thinking, *who is this asshole that he can sit there and decide whether I can succeed in the university or not? What does he know about me and what I am capable of accomplishing? He has no idea how hard I must work every day just to come to school. He has no idea that I have two jobs, one before school and one after school, on top of taking care of my younger brothers and sisters and all the family stuff because my father is at work.*

I looked into Mr. Wilson's eyes and yelled, "F**k you. I will go to the university if I want. I don't want to be a mechanic." Then I got up and walked away, shaking with anger.

Yes, I was a dreamer! And I just made sure that I would not graduate from high school. I had no idea what he would do, nor did I care. I wasn't that bad of a student if you consider that I was involved in athletics, such as football and track. When I wasn't at practice, I was working. I went to work at 5:30 in the morning, finished unloading trucks at Sears by 7:30, and was at school by 8. After football practice, I went home to make sure my sisters were okay, and that dinner was ready for my dad. Once my father arrived, I could go kicking around. With all the responsibility I carried as a young man and the busy schedule I kept; I was fortunate to get a C average. What I did know was how to work and be responsible.

In the fall, I enrolled at Blue Mountain Community College. In my first quarter, I got a 3.5 average. However, I could not afford to continue because my dad was too poor to help me. Living day-to-day and providing for a family on top of paying for college was more than one parent could manage alone. My education was my problem to figure out, and the only way out was to volunteer for the Army and to be able to get to use the GI Bill. I had heard about the GI Bill for as long as I can remember through my father and uncles who had served in World War II. None of them ever used GI Bill, but they talked about it. I understood it would pay for my education.

All the kids I had gone to high school with seemed to be going for more education. I was sure they got help from their parents or some sort of scholarship. No one in my family had ever gone to college; in fact, my brother and I were the first to graduate from high school. There was no one to turn to who could guide me on what to do or whom I could go to for help.

It was difficult to meet with my friends like we used to do, especially during the holidays when they were on break and having to listen to their stories of adventures at some faraway school. I understood that my future might not be like that. Indeed, it would never be like that unless I figured out a way to raise some money.

Beyond the question of money, my girlfriend Linda thought that because I had been going to the community college for one quarter, I had been chasing girls there. She issued an ultimatum. She wanted me to quit college, and if I didn't, we would have to break up. It was inconceivable to me that I could give up my dream of going to college and becoming a schoolteacher. On the other hand, how could I live without the person that I loved so much? I could not face my father and tell him I had given up. Why is it that teenagers have so many difficult choices?

On a cold fall morning just before Thanksgiving, my thoughts began to wander on the twenty-mile drive to college. In the past, my early morning drives usually meant that I was either going to class or a party up in the mountains for the weekend. The drive usually took twenty-five minutes, even in heavy traffic at seventy-five miles per hour. This Monday, it seemed as if it was never going to end, driving down the same freeway and looking for all the local landmarks that let me know how close I was to arriving or where the state police would be hiding to catch speeders like me. Of course, the state police rarely ticketed any of the locals who took I-84 because we knew where the traps were.

This Monday morning was different; the weekly routine would not apply. What was normal to do might never happen again. The rules and expectations that had become a part of my routine would soon cease to exist. This day would mark the beginning of another journey that would take me closer to the truth of the beginning, my roots.

CHAPTER 15
Uncle Sam

At the end of the day, we can endure much more than we think we can.
~ Frida Kahlo

I had already gone further than any member of our family by graduating from high school and attending one semester of community college. Fate had a different destiny for me, and my thoughts raced in many different directions. It was not obvious that my path had been carved into the ancient stones of my ancestors. My life would be a hard one with knowledge earned through pain. The road for me would not be to learn of the grants and scholarships that were available but never offered or discussed with me.

Mr. Wilson was right. I might never graduate from college, not because I lacked the will or ability but because I didn't have the money. There was nowhere to turn, and I didn't have a rich aunt or uncle, and that asshole Mr. Wilson would dance in delight to learn of my failure. Information is valuable. Information can control who gets an education and who doesn't. *Fuck-me! They won't be able to stop my dream no matter how long it takes*, I thought.

With the frustration of being broke and not knowing where to turn, random thoughts bombarded me until I was overcome with the curiosity of the wandering spirit. Suddenly, like my ancestors, I knew it was time to set out on my journey, search for my place, seek the truth. and find what was on the other side of those snow-capped mountains that I stared at every day from the student union. I had to go out into the world on my own, away from the protection of what I had always known—the familiarity and my family and friends. My first love had broken up with me. I chose college, and I wanted to get away anyway. There was no reason for me to stay.

I decided to drive downtown to the local pool hall with a friend to play a few games. We were there for a couple of hours, laughing and joking until boredom set in. We decided it was time to get back to our classes, but that is not what I did. As I drove past the Army recruiting office, I knew it was time for me to take my first step toward manhood like my father and my uncles. It was time for me to enter the ranks and face a warrior's fear, to learn how to overcome the challenges of fear, allowing it to become part of me, use it to make me stronger and to understand what people before me had sacrificed.

Since that Thanksgiving Day in 1969, I have had recurring thoughts of meeting my internal fears for the first time and accepting my rage. At nineteen, I knew I would be leaving home to change the rest of my life. That Thanksgiving dinner was unlike any other. I felt uneasy—an anxiety that has come only once in my lifetime. How would I break the news to my family? I decided to announce my decision that I enlisted at the dinner table and braced myself for the reaction.

I knew that strangers would soon take over my life, and I would not know who would be in charge or for what reason, just that control would not be mine. What was clear, however, was that death might be mine because of my spontaneous decision and my personal sense of manhood, which was leading me down a path of no return. Enlisting in the military was not something you could quit if you didn't like it. Once I signed the contract, I belonged to the Army. The men in my family, the men I looked up to, would recall the same feelings from time to time. I could only guess that everyone who chose this path had those feelings after signing up to become a warrior in an unknown war and in an unknown country.

Why, then, if I was already aware of these feelings and had heard all the same questions before, did the same thing happen to me? Even as the fear amplified in my mind all during Thanksgiving dinner, my time for leaving was drawing near and the answers I was hoping to get seemed to evade me. I still recall the smell of locust wood burning in the fireplace. We always looked for locust trees when we cut wood for the winter. It seemed to burn longer, and my father felt it was the best. The smell of the burning wood mixed with the cooking of turkey and dressing filled the house with the comfort of family conversations.

As I sat in the living room listening to those conversations and enjoying the different tantalizing smells of American food and Mexican dishes, my thoughts drifted to rage, thinking about leaving this comfortable home for a place I had never spotted on the map. Within the next two weeks, I would have to make my first trip alone to Portland. During the many trips there with my father, I never thought the day might come when it might be a final trip through the Columbia Gorge. The drive through the Gorge was always a reminder of the magnitude and power of God's ability to create beauty with the strength of the river behind it and the blend of rust, tan, green, and blues of the sky and the rocks. The beauty of the river reflected from its mirrored waters was an eternal reminder of our place on this earth. We are only a small part of what exists in the universe. God! It is beautiful!

God's Nature

Sitting on the riverbank

Seagulls fly.

Sturgeons jet.

Toward turquoise skies.

Fishing poles in hands

Movies created with images.

McDonald's hamburgers and Kentucky fried chicken.

Laughter of frozen memories.

Parents scream at children.

Stay out of the kitchen!

Playing football in the rodeo grounds

Swallowing horse shit!

Young men growing up.

Knowing just how far to take it!

Mothers' screams

Tears scaring their faces.

Dreaming of sons

Education and future places.

Young men chasing women.

Driving fast cars, dancing on death.

Mothers sitting in the living room.

Biting their fingernails,

Holding their breath.

Young men become fathers.

Babies scratch their faces.

Dreaming of daughters and future places.

Mothers grown old.

Spears in their hearts

Knowing that their family would grow apart.

I sat on the living room couch after dinner, listening to the conversations mixed with English and Spanish. Thoughts of being a hero or a coward hurled themselves through my brain. I was possessed by uncontrollable thoughts that conflicted with each other with no logic or reason to them.

How would I respond if I had to kill another person my age? God had not prepared me for the difficult choices I would soon have to face, dealing with the contradiction of my spiritual and religious beliefs in the church and the reality of life. Would I detach myself from my spiritual beliefs of worshipping all living creatures, or could I kill another nineteen-year-old fighting for his country, fighting for freedom, and fighting for a country that they believed in the same as I did? Could I shoot someone who listened to the same kind of music, who had a girlfriend and dreams of going to college? It wasn't difficult to imagine what he might look like. I could see what the mortality looked like on the evening news. I could turn on the television and see them lying dead on some dirt road in the middle of the jungle.

The pictures were close-ups. All I could think about as I saw the young dead Vietnamese bodies being dragged onto a dump truck was that they must have had a family that would mourn them and a girlfriend who would end up being with someone else because they chose to be a warrior like their people before them.

Reality

High school dreams,

Driving fast cars

Cruising the gut,

Drinking beer from paper cups.

Squealing tires,

Chasing pretty girls,

Hair blowing in the soft desert wind.

Main streetlights of green, yellow, and red

Flashing unexpected warnings to youth.

Weekend keggers

On a riverbank's edge,

Campfires burning

Rock and roll exploding.

Silence broken like a shattered window.

Amplified by the river's glossy back.

Stories whispered,

Between songs of tomorrow.

What will you be when you grow up?

Classrooms filled with smiling faces.

Reckless as young colts without firm legs.

News of war flashes

The evening news

Parents smoke cigarettes, drink coffee.

Kill ratios interrupt the family dinner.

Brothers and sisters argue over washing dishes.

Young men making plans in the restroom.

A weekend dance,

Dreams of kissing a sweetheart.

Caressing a breast,

Experience life in love.

A child's voyage is unknown.

At eighteen comes graduation.

Spring brings its cool rains,

Trees bring leaves,

Heat waves rise from highways.

Fears of opening doors,

Dark rooms of the future.

Unknown footsteps,

A first letter of greeting arrives,

Physical examinations

In forbidden cities.

Who is Uncle Sam?

On that Thanksgiving Day, after my girlfriend left me for someone else, it was my turn to become the typical story behind a country western song. Of course, it could never have been anything related to the reckless behavior of an angry Latino with a chip on his shoulder. Regardless of what I would face in the days to follow, Portland was my destination four days before my birthday.

Volunteering for military service was always part of a plan devised long before my time and agreed to by a nineteen-year-old who felt that the only risk in volunteering to serve was not returning to use the educational benefits after my discharge. A fair exchange, I thought: two years in the Army for a college education. My only sacrifice would be to risk going to Vietnam and getting killed. Somehow, logical reasoning never entered my decision and the impact it would have if the worst happened.

Many young men my age carried the same sense of invincibility as well as the same urgency to break the cycle of poverty they were born into. It seemed that at nineteen, nothing could kill you. Only the other guy would get killed or paralyzed. Death is something that would happen to someone else in a faraway place; it could never happen to me.

My plan was to spend two years in the Army, get an early out, go back to Blue Mountain Community College, and then go to the University of Oregon. It was difficult to see any fault in this brilliant plan devised by a borderline genius, but there was a major flaw. It was 1969 when young men were fleeing the United States and going to Canada to avoid the draft, refusing to take part in a war that had no purpose to the citizens of this country, especially the youth. It was extremely difficult for citizens of Hermiston, Oregon, a town of 4,500, to believe that they would personally benefit from the war in Vietnam. What could be the possible benefit from a war thousands of miles away?

My future was laid out before me. All I had to do was go to Portland and pass the physical. I was afraid that the physical would find a defect and keep me from getting in. My older brother Gerardo had failed his physical six months earlier when they found too much sugar in his blood and noted him as a borderline diabetic. How could too much sugar in my blood keep me from being a good soldier? Damn! It seemed like such a good plan!

Anxiety became a close friend as the time moved closer to my physical date. I had heard so many stories as a young boy from my uncles who had lived through the experience and from friends who had signed up even before they graduated from high school. Everyone who had gone to Portland for a physical came back with a unique story. They described the horrors of taking the physical with a recognizable uneasiness in a room filled with forty or fifty other guys standing naked in two lines with their backs to each other, having to bend over and grab their ankles while someone in uniform walked down the center of the room, looking up their ass.

I could never figure out what they were looking for. Why would anyone have to look up your ass, especially if you were only joining the Army? What would be up your ass that would keep you from being a good soldier? It seems like some kind of perversion to have to expose your body to everyone just to become a soldier. All I needed was to be able to run, march, and shoot. At least, that is how it was done in the movies, and that was how it sounded talking to some of my friends.

Standing in line, I faced another lengthy line of men as the doctor walked by, checking everyone for hernias. I realized that the Army would not be my protector or guardian. How dehumanizing to have some sergeants walk around, screaming at us and calling us maggots, and instructing us to let someone look up our ass, and then push on our balls with forty other people watching. There was no way of knowing what to expect as I slipped back and forth from reality into daydreams like the silent black-and-white movies. At least the thought of home was warm and comfortable with the sounds of family and the smells of familiar foods; at least during the fantasy, I could feel comfort. I could keep things the same in my mind. I would never have to leave my girlfriend, my buddies would all be hanging on the same block, and our house would always be warm and full of laughter. In my mind, nothing would change.

I didn't have to wait long to find out what fate would bring me. At the end of the day, I was told to get ready to ship out to Fort Lewis. I had fully expected to go home for a couple of weeks and then report to base. But things had changed, and they were shipping people out as soon as they passed their physical. We were taken to a room with red carpeting and an American flag next to a podium where a drill sergeant administered the oath to support the Constitution. As we were preparing to take our oath, an unexpected event unfolded, something I'd never heard of from my father, uncles, or anyone else who had been through the induction process. Just as we thought we were moments away from taking our oath, a Marine sergeant entered the room and announced, "Today is your lucky day; we are going draft five Marines today." He explained that everyone's name had been placed in a hat, and five would be drawn to receive the distinct honor of becoming Marines.

As the sergeant finished speaking, a voice from the back of the room rang out, "You can't take me; I wear girls' panties!" I turned to see who had spoken and recognized a guy from a small town fifteen miles away from Hermiston. Despite the outburst, he wasn't selected to become a Marine but still had to report for duty that day. I no sooner had repeated the oath than I was on my way to Fort Lewis.

Upon arriving at Fort Lewis, a team of greeters were waiting as we arrived, we pulled into the parking lot and the bus driver opened the door, and then three men dressed in uniform started screaming obscenities at us to get off the bus and get in formation. Hell, I had no idea what formation meant. But it did not take long for me to find out that smiling, laughing, and joking was not a positive trait. This became my greatest challenge as I am someone with a permanent smile. What was worse was that the more pain or pressure I felt, the bigger my smile got.

During the first few days, I was continuously reminded that I was less than human and that my life was no longer mine. After a couple of weeks, we heard there was a national lottery, and people were getting drafted. All I could think about was my friends, and I prayed they would not end up here having to learn these early lessons.

The rumors were true. A few weeks after my departure from Hermiston, on a cold December night, the Selective Service held a lottery designed to randomly draft people by birth date. It was a big deal, but it could not affect me personally as I was already in. However, I was interested in finding out the dates because of my friends back home. I was sure that Ben would buy some beer, invite some friends, and watch the lottery drawing on television. I am sure that he got one of our buddies, who was twenty-one, to buy him a case of Miller, that beautiful gold liquid in the clear bottle. The case lasted the entire night, and it would have turned into a big party. But the party would be short-lived. No sooner did it get started than they drew a birth date that my buddies knew; December 6 was the tenth number drawn, and it was my date. Suddenly it became real to them and it was clear that this might not be a time to party.

Life suddenly became more serious for my friends, too, with shorter periods of time carrying greater meaning. If it were only possible to slow time down and take forever before another birth date was called. Maybe the war would end before they reached their numbers. Later I talked with my friends, who described the wrenching feeling that tightened their stomachs into a knot, turning their disbelief, fantasy, and loneliness into a reality. We all asked, "How could this be?" What would our destiny be: to go to war and die? What was that expression that my dad said from time to time? Only the good die young, or he was too mean to die. Either way, I was too young, and now I wanted to be mean. It wouldn't pay to be good. On the other hand, wouldn't it be a violation of the Ten Commandments to kill someone? Could the church help us with this? Desperation was setting in.

When I finally got to see Ben while I was on leave, he stared into my eyes as if he were wondering what to say to me, but there was nothing to say. I got up slowly from the chair, and for the first time I could remember, I wanted to get away from Ben and not be around anyone who had fallen victim to this awful thing that our country was doing to us. I wanted to be alone to figure out what had happened to my friends. As for me, I had made my choice, and it was not imposed on me.

Walking out of Ben's house, I thought, *I hope Ben comes out all right.* I wasn't worried about Robert; he had failed his physical, and besides, he had managed to get a criminal record. Thank God for the police! Bill was another friend of the police and would not have any problem staying home.

As I got down the driveway and into my pickup, numbness came over my body. My truck made a grinding sound as I tried to start it while it was running. I put it in gear and drove off in a daze, not knowing what to do. I drove for hours; to this day I don't know where I went.

Driving without a destination was my way of running away from the stark truth that I would soon have to face my fate when I returned to base. Every evening, the reality of the news reports on television forced its way into my thoughts as I drove around wondering how I could have been number ten in the lottery. How could I even know what a kill ratio was? Why would I want to know how many Vietnamese had been killed that day? As I stopped at the only intersection in town with a traffic light, I realized I didn't even know where Vietnam was. Who cares what they do to themselves, and how could they be threatening America if I don't even know where they live? How could they expect me to just show up and go to some country that I don't know anything about and kill people who had done nothing to me?

I had never had to think about killing or dying before. After a couple of hours, I realized that I could not drive away from what had just happened to all of us. I knew that my only choice was to do what my father and uncles had done. The lottery would have made no difference to me. It only reinforced a decision that had already been made the day I was born. There was no way out. My family would expect me to serve, and I needed the GI Bill to go to college. The only thing left to do was to go back after my leave.

Finally, I got the courage to go back to Ben's house. His birth date came up number 366. I could not believe it! He got the extra day for leap year. What luck! He wouldn't have to go at all. With that number, he wouldn't even have to go to college to stay out of the service.

It was hard to imagine what I would face when I got back. Memories only allowed me to think of my father waking me in the middle of the night with his screams of fear from the ghosts of war and watching him shivering in his bed from the malaria that he brought home. There had always been a distant look in his eyes; sometimes, I thought that it was a look of guilt, the kind of look that I get when I think I have committed a sin against God. He was not alone. I could see the same distance between my Uncle Jose and my Uncle Francisco. Would I end up the same or could I avoid it by knowing in advance that it could happen?

The war created many ghosts for the men who raised me and served as my role models. They carried with them the haunting atrocities of war until their deaths. Had God really wanted my father to be a killer at eighteen? Did my country really want me to be a killer at nineteen? Was it possible that our country intended to train an entire army of men capable of forgetting their Christian morality and killing other human beings, and then, when the war was over, retrain them into understanding that it is not okay to kill? They were at war one day and on the street looking for a job the next. In the case of my father and uncles, they served as good Americans fighting for the country they believed in and for the principles and values that it stood for. While they were in, they were soldiers, and as soon as they were released, they became spics all in the time that it took to type the DD 214, giving them their official military discharge. There were spics in every community throughout America. Now it was my turn to make the same decisions.

Everyone pays a price in war. What isn't clear are the rewards bestowed on those who have given themselves to their country and the price they continue to pay upon their return. Did my father and those in my family who served receive the same treatment and benefits as those Anglo soldiers who returned from battle? Were they received with the same enthusiasm in the unemployment lines as those with fair skin, blond hair, and blue eyes? Even as a child, I recognized that my family had given much to become part of this great nation, yet I have always known that we were not welcome. What would be the reason for spending almost five years in the Pacific fighting for your country, only to return to America to work as a migrant laborer?

Recognizing that we had been left out of the equation as a community, I still felt that I had to serve. After all, we came from a people of warriors. The spirit of the past still haunted our presence and seemed to be guiding our future in searching for this land for the truth.

A little over twenty years later, my generation saw history repeat itself. Many young men in the prime of their youthful rebellion had their lives disrupted and changed forever because of the 1969 lottery that cold December evening. Those who came before us from the hidden populations paid a greater price when they served for what they believed. They believed in a nation of freedom and equality. But they received violence against their neighborhoods and their communities as a gift of gratitude.

Betrayal

Dark blue-gray skies

Sprinkling holy water

Over a dry earth.

Chilled air creating

Smoke signals on the horizon.

Steaming off human lips.

Fear! Rage!

Pouring into my watery eyes,

Taking a silent ride

In the back of a 1967 Pontiac

Fear! Rage!

Pounding through my chest,

Trembling arms,

Turning in my stomach.

Fear! Rage!

Stealing youthful laughter.

A young boy is ready to die.

Leaving abroad,

Clinching a father's advice.

Out of that 1967 Pontiac

A man steps out.

Leaving youth forever behind!

Robbed! Eternity!

A young warrior boards.

A blue, red, gray chariot.

A Greyhound waits

Prepared for battle.

Rock and roll sounds, a prayer.

Stories of sweethearts left behind.

Love that was in passing

Love that could be with life.

Ready to ride this chariot.

Fear! Rage!

Squeezing my gut

Tears accepting the silent

Would-be warrior,

A soldier in boy's clothing,
Ready to empty my soul of love.
Staring out of the Greyhound
Bus window to the future,
Knowing with clenched fists
To have love is to lose love.
In battle, if I have nothing
I lose nothing!
Empty now!
As I stare at the foggy window,
Carefully clearing a circular opening,
Spying on my family,
The chariot begins to roll toward.
Fear! Rage!
Away from love,
Love for a girl I should marry.
A high school sweetheart fade
As the fog crawls onto the road.
Fear! Rage!
Burst into a small tear!

As the child peeks

Through warrior's eyes

Fear! Rage!

Take control.

I am only nineteen years old. Why me?

I don't want to die.

Where is Vietnam?

Who says this is important?

When you have nothing

You lose nothing.

Fear! Rage!

Become my companion.

God will be my guardian.

Everything I had been taught by my father, aunts, and uncles led me to a decision that would change my life forever. The lessons passed on to me about loyalty, pride in living in this country, and the gratitude that I should have for the opportunity to earn a living, regardless of how meager, guided my decision to volunteer in the Army.

We always had food to eat and a place to live, keeping us out of the rain, so why should we complain? We just need to work harder, my Tia Rico would say. She always believed in this country. Her belief in America stemmed from her life as an orphan with eight siblings to raise during a time after the revolution in Mexico when going to America was the only salvation from hunger and the atrocities that war delivers on the doorsteps of the helpless. Oh yes, she believed, and she always made sure that we obeyed all the laws and did not make any waves. It was her job to make sure we believed in what this country made available and that we took advantage of it.

The need to search for my place of destiny remained like a dark shadow on an otherwise bright sunny day, clinging to the one who gives it life. The being that gave birth to the shadow is the other side of the shadow that behaves like a Siamese twin, mimicking every movement. The contrast between the brightness of sunshine and the darkness of the elusive shadow brings with it the answers to many of the mysteries in my life. In searching for those answers, there seems to be a force from behind pushing me to move forward.

Was it the truth, or just a need to find a place of belonging? A solution to the wandering in my heart, or is it just the confusion of a young boy becoming a man? Military experience was part of it but not the final place of truth, and it did not provide the evidence that my ancestors searched for and left for us to find. Two years in the Army gave me an education but not one that could be gained at a university; this education was much more costly. My memories include a suicide attempt by a young man whose fear of dying by another hand was great enough that he was willing to kill himself. Or my roommate from Philadelphia, who I found sitting on the floor eating shoe wax because he had taken too many drugs.

Drugs were everywhere, but then it was 1969 and who hadn't had a taste of the forbidden? The drug of choice was good, strong pot (la marijuana), and the imported stuff was always in demand. The American was just okay, but the stuff from Thailand could make you hallucinate. Mexican pot was always good and only got better. It was not always satisfying to smoke a little pot or drink a little whisky. Someone always wanted to get a little higher, which meant the chemicals.

Acid was the journey maker; we could always count on a

good trip, but we were never guaranteed that everyone would come back. There was never a choice to go to customer service and complain because one of our buddies did not return from their trip in the same condition they left. We lost a few along the way.

Sadness fills my heart at the thought of my buddies. We became such close friends, and they touched my heart. My writing of them in memory is a testament that they touched me forever and the emptiness that has been left lingering within. Yes, some were my friends. When you are nineteen, it is easy to love in many ways without knowing that love is also accompanied by heartbreak. Is anyone counting all the casualties from drugs like they count the ones from war? There were so many drugs to take, and it didn't help when the men who served as your officers, the lieutenants and captains, would give you drugs and ask you for drugs.

One of my captains used my room to get loaded. Innocence became a thing of the past, and survival became the soul of the present because where there are a lot of drugs, you also begin to see paranoia. If you weren't doing some shit, you were a narc. The Black soldiers hung with themselves, the Latinos were also separate, and neither group trusted the Whites. Mistrust, anger, and paranoia were rampant to the point that blanket parties were given on behalf of those who were suspected of being narcs. No one ever waited for proof.

How could we have fought a war when everyone I knew was loaded? Was it possible that I just got put in a unit with alcoholics and junkies? Oh God, where was my innocence? I got cheated out of being a boy. I had once enjoyed being a boy, and I wanted it to last forever. Please let me have some of that back.

An angel sent a lieutenant colonel from Louisiana to serve as my protector in Germany. On my first day in Germany, Colonel Watts came into the receiving area, asking for me by name from a list he held in his hand. He stood silently, studying the sheet of paper, which I knew had information on me and what I had done in the past. Then, in a soft voice, he asked if there was a man by the name of Vasquez in the room.

Dear God, here it comes. My duty station will be cleaning out the toilets in the barracks. "Yes, that is me, Sir," my mouth blurted out without any prompting from my mind.

Colonel Watts looked at me for a moment and asked in a soft but sincere voice, "How would you like to become my battalion mail clerk and serve as my personal driver?"

In shock, my only reaction was that it must be some form of punishment or some kind of special duty that placed me in harm's way. I had no idea what I would have to do to be the colonel's driver. Is it possible that he wanted to help me? If so, what was this Anglo trying to do to me? After all, we had just arrived. I did not have enough time to cause any trouble. My instincts said that it was something to jump on immediately.

"Yes, it would be an honor, Sir."

That job became my permanent duty station in Wurzburg, and I was exempt from morning formation and any added duty. The colonel also let me drive his personal car on weekends for special occasions such as a hot date, and he gave me advice when he felt it was necessary. The most important thing he ever did for my survival was to refuse to sign my three requests for transfer to Vietnam. On the third request, he called me into his office and began by saying that no matter how many times my request for Vietnam crossed his desk, he would continue to reject it. He said that Vietnam was not a place for men like me and that I had more important things to do than to waste away in a jungle fighting an unknown enemy. How he knew what things remained to be done in my life was beyond my comprehension.

Colonel Watts had information he felt was better not shared with me and chose never to discuss his knowledge of my future and the challenges it would bring. Only he had the answers as to why he had singled me out for special treatment without ever conveying it to me and without ever knowing who I was or where I came from.

As young men can, my speculation was that he had served in Vietnam with someone named Vasquez, who may have saved his life or at least done a great deed to deserve the appreciation that was passed on to me. How odd it seemed that for the first time in my life, an Anglo had taken steps to be kind to me. And what was even more difficult to understand was that this White man was treating me with special privilege. It only seemed natural to draw the conclusion that he owed someone with the same last name as mine a debt of gratitude, and he made me the recipient.

Colonel Watts not only protected me from the unknown; without his help, it would have been especially difficult for me to deal with authority when I had grown up with the freedom of traveling throughout the country with little supervision or guidance. I've always had a clear understanding of who I was, or at least that's what I thought. During times of confusion, such as I experienced in the military, I had to remind myself of the beginning of my people and the importance of learning from every experience and search for the value and the truth of them. Does the truth really exist, and if so, where might I find it?

The greatest price of all was the little bit of innocence that remained untouched by the bitter truth of the ability people had to lose respect for themselves and their families and everything that their heritage stood for. If they did not have this, what was left? Learning about the challenges in life always brings with it a greater price. You can't buy a true-life experience at a bargain store. The price could not be paid for with scholarships or by getting the GI Bill. It could only be obtained by paying the tuition for living through it and it is not always the pleasant experience a nineteen-year-old expects from life. Life learning comes with the price tag of sacrifice, which could have been the ultimate price in 1969. In a sense, achieving my goal of obtaining the truth of what to do next and where to go had been carried out, at least for the time being.

My experience taught me what I didn't want to do and where I didn't want to go. The two years in the Army became my guidance counselors pointing me in the right direction. The Indian blood running through my veins pushed me beyond the snow-covered mountains to a new world of knowledge, hardship, and a clearer understanding of how I must move forward and out of the maze that surrounded me. Somewhere in all of this were some lessons to capture and preserve.

Fort Dix, New Jersey. I recall thinking what a dump! However, this was the place that would release me back into the world. How did we all get here? Where did we all come from? Is it possible that all these men had been here three days waiting for the first person in a position of authority and wearing a pickle suit (an Army uniform) to walk in into the hall where at least three hundred soldiers were waiting in line for their orders—orders that would finally allow them to go home. The men had waited a lifetime, or so it seemed, to be released from active duty. I guess the Army thought another few hours would not make a difference. No one could leave the military without permission. To go home for good—oh God, what a wonderful thought! To be able to live a life not dictated every minute of the day by someone in a green uniform. *Stuck here for almost three days going from line to line with the other men, or are we men?*

CAMP SONG

American's patriots arrive, symbolic of distinct
cultural strongholds.

West, Northwest, Mississippi Delta, Appalachia,
Southwest Border,

Hurry, and wait, orders coming, a predetermined
fate, jungle, or desert!

Months of training, unprepared to prepare them,
will they survive,

look at each other, thoughts racing, imaginary
conclusions,

Heros of causality, standing in formation, a
winding snake like line,

Twelve hundred men long, restless, anxiety
discovers a nervous tick,

Not knowing, they question who will tell us, eye
twitching,

crazy leg shaking, silence, waiting in silent prayer,
three hours pass,

1200 soldiers Dressed in pickle green uniforms,

endless hours pass, same line same spot, no
change five hours pass,

in deafening silence, eight hours pass, encouraged
anger invades.

The silent pickle line, twelve hours pass,

rebellion creeps into well trained minds,

Sunrise to sunset, no orders, no movement,

Confirmation no orders coming,

ahh, finally, a pickle suit, two silver bars
shouldered,

sunset arrives, Unanswered questions,

Commands to abandon the snake line,

A military meal prepared by nineteen-year-old chefs,

not ready for canned meals

Twelve hundred warriors anxious, angry, ready for fate,

silence rules,

well-trained men, thoughtful silence dominates,

where will we go? Jungle or desert,

What will they do? Who will come back?

Two a.m. a thunderous eruption of sound explodes.

in the midnight air, a song fills the empty echoes,

projecting the sound of soul of an unknown soldier,

"Summertime and the living is easy."

An unknown patriot releases his soul for all to hear.

into the dark of midnight

for all, the living is easy for now, waiting for the final duty station,

A soulful song bouncing off barracks walls, echoing across the camp,

A space of imagination, orders do not matter,

Their paths have been mapped; fate is drawn.

At twenty-one, it's still hard to feel like a man when my thoughts are those of a young boy out of high school. On reflection, it is hard to imagine our country truly needed eighteen-year-old children to fight its war. Is it in the best interest of this nation to send young men to war when they have not matured enough to make life-and-death decisions? How could our nation's leaders send young boys to war? Didn't I hear somewhere that the average age of the men who fought in World War II was twenty-seven? Why weren't they helping this time?

Was Vietnam so different? In 1969, at nineteen, being drafted was the only thing left to do when your birth date on the lottery list had come up. Waiting in line for my release, I could see the new recruits walking by toward a life they had no understanding of. Those new recruits looked even younger. It was hard to imagine that they could draft eighteen-year-olds. They all looked like children. In the time I served I had matured beyond my actual years. Those new kids waiting to process in seemed less mature and more sheltered than I was when I volunteered.

Life in the military gave me an understanding of the fear in a person that makes him able to resign everything important in life to chance or fate. The fate that hopefully would bring us home exactly the way we left. But we learned that that is impossible because our lives changed once we agreed to serve because of the choices we had made to get in and what we had to do to get out.

It was difficult to imagine what had happened in the United States or the "real world," as we got used to calling it. No one knew what to expect after they were released. Waiting for those fools to process us out was just another reminder of what the last two years had been like and that getting out was my best choice. Coming home should have been the greatest moment of my life. Instead, it forced me to understand the ease with which people can allow themselves to hate.

My earlier understanding of hatred was driven by having been with Anglos who hated us because we were Mexican. The thought of hating the warriors who go off to defend your lands, cities, and everything that makes up what you belong to was incomprehensible. What kind of hatred is this that allows people to deliberately plan the surrounding of cities next to the great Aztec capitol, leading to the eventual destruction of the kingdom and murdering of hundreds of people?

How could an entire country lose so much respect for itself in such a short time? There was no respect left for the children who were returning from war alone with no one to greet them. Many young men and women returned from serving this great nation only to hide their uniforms and conceal from their closest friends that they had served during the war. There grew an internal conflict in me around what my family had raised me to believe in and what was being practiced on the streets all over America.

Somehow, while traveling from Fort Dix, New Jersey to Portland Oregon, hate did not reveal its ugly head until my first steps off the Greyhound and onto Burnside Avenue in Portland. Two young people walked toward me, noticing my uniform. Instead of greeting me with a smile and hello, they hurled insults and spit was catapulted from their tiny angry faces, hitting their target. Baby Killer! They seemed so vicious, as if they wanted to kill me. Their bodies had stiffened with hatred as if rigor mortis had already set in.

To this day, no greater sadness has touched my soul more than finding out for the first time that what some of my friends died for what seemed to have no value to the people of this country. Yet the hatred that glared from the eyes of those two young people could only have been the same type of hatred that the soldiers of the Conquista had been exposed to—hatred that spread through the veins of the Spanish soldiers during the massacres of the Indians as they killed women, children, and the warriors who faced them.

The incident in Portland reminded me of what my uncles experienced in Los Angeles after World War II. They talked of a hot muggy summer in 1943, typical of Los Angeles summers. You could hear music blaring from the brightly painted homes in shades of turquoise and salmon, decorating the landscape like you would find in many Mexican communities. Music was everywhere; it was like being transported to a neighborhood in Mexico City. The homes had been built a section at a time as the money would allow or as the family grew. Homes were constructed out of need and not to keep one step ahead of the Garcias.

Hundreds of thousands of young Chicano men came back from the war and faced the challenge of rebuilding their lives. My father had been gone for five years without ever coming home, and overnight, he was back, facing the prospect of finding a job and re-establishing relationships with loved ones he hadn't seen in all that time.

This country was full of Chicano warriors who had just returned from the war still wearing their medals of honor, their silver stars, bronze stars, and campaign ribbons, aching for peace and the love of their family. If bravery is measured by medals earned in time of war, the Chicano warrior was the bravest. Those who fought next to us know firsthand the meaning of courage.

The time had come for the Chicano, the Mexican American, Latino, or whatever the Anglo population wanted to call us to have a place we could call home. As a culture, we earned the right to be called Americans if that is what we wanted. Chicano men left their homes as boys and returned as men with a new sense of belonging and with an expectation of what they had earned for their families. They could no longer be content with eating only where greasers or spics were allowed. They returned home with a determination to assume their place in this country that was promised to everyone willing to make the ultimate sacrifice. There was an unwritten contract made with each soldier who had served. Now it was time to have that contract fulfilled.

But this was not to be the case. Society had not caught up with the notion that everyone was equal regardless of the sacrifice. There still seemed to be some unwritten law that if you were of any color other than White, you had to abide by different rules and laws—a conflict in expectations between what had existed before the war and what should have been after the war.

Times had changed without providing enough notification for those most affected. History was rewriting its pages, and the script had been written before anyone had time to read it. There was nothing left but for the two to clash. America's society was ready to clash with itself and the promises it had made to people who were ready for the change, and it had failed to inform the segment of society that would have to share some of its benefits that had traditionally been held solely for their consumption. How could anyone predict the pain that would be caused by expecting people to share the pursuit of life, liberty, and happiness with certain inalienable rights?

The Chicano was focused on equality, equity, and democracy, ideals for which they had risked their lives while serving in several wars and through multiple generations. After all, they had had plenty of time to think about them while they were in the trenches, wondering if their time would come up.

America was not ready for what it had created. Then in June of 1943, the story of an incident in Los Angeles was shared from Colonia to Colonia and state to state in our neighborhoods. Not one single barrio escaped the news of the atrocity committed against our community. It was as if war had been declared against all people of Latino descent, especially the

Chicano. Was it possible that expecting equality and freedom, we were expecting too much. The story spread through the camps as well.

After the war, after our warriors had come home, the city of Los Angeles declared war on a barrio, and hundreds of U.S. military personnel went on a search-and-destroy mission through East Los Angeles and the downtown area of the city. They assaulted any Chicanos they came across, tearing their clothes off if they wore anything that resembled a Zoot suit. These fashionable outfits included a pair of fine baggy slacks topped by a long coat the length of an overcoat and decorated with a long key chain hanging from the belt loops into the pocket and topped by a huge pork pie hat. The attacks were deliberate, violent, and without reason.

Of course, there had been no official declaration of war, no violated treaties, or broken laws. The only criteria for attack were a Zoot suit or a young Chicano. The war went on for over a week, although it seemed like a lifetime. All of this had gone on without one single finger lifted by local law enforcement to come to the aid of the citizens who had been attacked in their own communities.

What crime had been committed? What about the contract for those who had served and protected the American values? Attacks occurred in other parts of the country, such as Oakland, San Diego, and Delano. Who will ever know how many attacks took place that were never reported? With this declaration of war, the Pachuchos did not go away; they only grew in numbers. We were no longer willing to just go along. They became stronger than ever, membership increasing out of a sense of community to protect the village, the barrio. What else could be expected when your sisters, mothers, fathers, brothers, and girlfriends were attacked without reason and in defiance of logic? The line had to be drawn for some.

In my circle of friends there were other casualties, too, among the friendships that were kept long after high school. Bill went to prison, something we could all have predicted. His anger was beyond repair and got only worse as time went on. We lost him to Wilma's love, who abandoned his passion, smiled at it, and left it broken. Prison became his fate.

John survived the brutality of Vietnam but went to live with amphetamines, used as aspirin for the pot highs, and he was a constant guest with heroin chased by a coke high. John brought back more than post-traumatic stress disorder. He also brought the chemicals invented by our government, Agent Orange, which invaded his body. John worked in the woods until a few years ago. Even though the forest helped him, it was not enough to survive his escapades, war, drugs, chemicals, and the challenges life that brought him. Yet, he is still the only true scholar I have ever known, quietly sitting at home reading about the world, at peace, single and alone with his soul.

Ben did not survive beyond twenty-two, meeting his fate on one of those country roads that we cruised as young boys. He used to travel that road with his arms around his sweetheart, dreaming of the next party and talking about war stories and his last romance. Ben died with heroin in his blood and Vietnam on his soul. The Army chewed up that soul and sent back a warrior without a war. God forgive this great nation for letting Ben go at such an early age. He was the peacemaker, a proud Ogalala warrior from Pine Ridge, South Dakota. Robert has survived life's trials and is working as a technician for a government agency. He is clean from the drugs and alcohol and fighting this world. He's still single, yes single, with four children from three different women.

As for me, I'm sitting here alone, writing down these thoughts before they change or, worse yet, before they disappear. After all, it's part of what I am supposed to do. I arrived at this place a stranger, made many friends, had many positive experiences but was never really accepted into the new world. I did, however, learn a unique way of life that allowed me greater understanding of how the new world could be transformed.

CHAPTER 16
Dreams Pursued

La vida es un sueño, y los sueños, sueños son.
(Life is a dream, and dreams are but dreams.)
~ Origin from the play *La vida es sueño* (*Life is a Dream*) by the Spanish playwright Pedro Calderón de la Barca.

Getting a degree had been internalized so deeply that the thought of not achieving that goal never occurred to me. As a young Chicano with high aspirations, with no support or advocacy on my behalf, achieving my goal at times seemed impossible. The driving force that allowed the dream to stay alive was the enduring support and love from family and members of the community. They believed in me and gave constant encouragement and reinforcement that it could be accomplished—*querer es poder* (to want to, is to be able to). In other words, they would say to me, "You must want it first. Then you can get there."

A young dreamer only needs to decide what they are going to be when they grow up. Painting was the only way imaginable for me to bare my soul for everyone to see without appearing weak to the tough guys who were part of my world. My immediate circle of friends had different aspirations that many times conflicted with my vision of myself. When I was with my friends, my weekends consisted of smoking weed, drinking, and cruising the gut. My buddies already perceived a weakness in me because of my interest in art. They had yet to learn that my other interest was writing poetry and learning about the world outside of our colonia. I couldn't imagine what their reactions would have been if they had known that I was writing love poems.

Love was a forbidden topic. God forbid that a man writes something about loving a woman so much that his heart would break him into tears. They could never know that my heart had been broken many times over love for a young woman who surfaced a passion of fire and ice in surging moments of simultaneous joy, pain, and fear. Art was the only way to hide the weakness and frailty that love, and passion can control us with. The dreamer in me still wanted to be a painter when I was twenty-one. It didn't matter what my buddies thought of my weakness. There was something inside of me that wanted out.

Cultivation of further learning became a tool that would help me open new doors to more choices. I reached a crossroads when it was time to leave the safety of military life, a life without daily decisions about what to wear to work, what to cook, or where to live. It was time to decide. I could have stayed in the military, which would have been easy. I had already reached a reasonable rank that provided an acceptable income. Or I could move on to the next challenge and start pursuing my education. It was not clear what direction to turn or what to become as an adult. What was clear, however, was my decision of what I did not want to do to make a living. I did not want to be a migrant farmworker or a soldier.

Like many other young Chicanos, my choices were difficult. If I chose to go home to be with my family, it would mean returning to life in a migrant labor camp. It would be a life of traveling from one small farm town to another, never knowing whether the work would be there or not. Work would never be certain. It would always depend on the weather or skill of the farmer to produce a good crop. Yet, while it would be a difficult way of life, we would always be together as a family. A second possibility, as I said, was to make the Army my career and have all my decisions made for me without the worry of surviving the day-to-day struggles that families all over the country face daily. Going to college away from my family was a third possible choice.

While these seemed to be difficult choices, the decision had already been made for me long before this crossroads. The decision was made by the old ones who wandered this country for hundreds of years, passing on the prophecy one person at a time and telling the stories of the ones here before us. It had been recognized by the curandera who healed me all those years earlier. She had foreseen my future within a few minutes and told me that education would be a part of my life, that my life would be surrounded by education, wealth, and work—a struggle for the people who loved me.

Maturing into adulthood brought with it a greater demand for knowledge and wisdom of life's struggle. A greater responsibility consumed my awareness of the inequities that surrounded the people who meant the most to me. An awakening had begun to take place inside my soul, to the point of possession and the creation of an internal revolt with my spirit fighting the practical world on earth against the spiritual world inside. And the spiritual part of my being that carries the strength of will always wins the conflict with the physical world.

This awakening brought to my awareness the fact that the families I had worked with from dusk to dawn, seven days a week, had to continue to live a lifestyle that is equal to, if not worse than, that of any third-world country. Entire families had to live in one-room shacks with no toilet or shower, large cracks and gaps in the walls that let in the daylight and didn't keep the weather out. One bed for two or three people and sometimes two to three beds per room, a wood stove for heating and cooking. These families suffer the harshness of the weather, work, and living conditions and are the same families that spend their lives cultivating and harvesting food for others to eat. How is it possible to harvest food all day twelve to fourteen hours a day and still go home hungry?

Some families would not even have the luxury of getting one of those wooden shacks because they had arrived in the camps too late, and all the shacks were taken. The place of last resort was to camp outside, cook over campfires, sleep in tents, or in your car every day.

How could America know that people were living under freeways, in tents, or along a railroad track with a campfire without eliminating such deplorable conditions? Is it that easy to ignore the labor camps without indoor plumbing, with waste running through the middle of the camp, and community showers for men, women, and children? Were we that invisible? Who was there to fight for the dignity of the children who carried the blood of kings, who were the descendants of pyramid builders, writers, scientists and, of course, artists?

Young Chicanos (Raza) from all over the country were beginning to ask the same questions and experiencing the same unrest coupled with an anger that had begun to boil throughout the community of young radicals who had already served in the military or received an education in some of the best universities in the country. It was as if everyone knew instinctively that the time was near. Modern warriors were coming home from the war with impatience at the neglect and abuse of a nation that had no difficulty asking its children to die for its founding principles, but that lacked the fortitude to make sure those same children were afforded all its luxuries. Simple luxuries, such as the freedom to get a good paying job, just like the Anglos who were coming home.

How about the ability to eat in any restaurant you choose or to be able to have a beer in any tavern you choose without having to fight your way to the bottom of the bottle. It was a time when impatience grew to violence because we were tired of being invisible.

We were no longer willing to receive our conquerors with

open arms as we did in the past when the Spaniards arrived on our shores. We could no longer look to the gods to protect us as a people. The signs had already become clear when our temples were torn down stone by stone by the Spaniards to build their churches. We stood silent because of what we knew in the prophecy. That prophecy would not protect our mothers from being violated and taken into the world that we have today. We can no longer stand by and watch the children being deprived of their ancient knowledge. Our souls have never been anything other than Indian, the great Aztec nation that was thrown into disarray because of small acts of kindness to a hidden enemy and a belief in what the future would bring.

The future is now, and we have returned to prepare ourselves for the journey back to ancient knowledge. Anger seemed to float in the air, settling in people's hearts and transforming itself into organized movements, a struggle. We were not alone; there were many others wanting to fight for the opportunity to live a life of freedom, to live where you wanted, go to school where you wanted, drink where you wanted, or just to be like everyone else. We never wanted to be White English-speaking blue-eyed blond-haired Americans. All we ever expected was to be able to have the same rights as everyone else, speak our language, worship freely, practice ancient customs, and most of all be able to live as Raza.

What is so difficult about allowing someone to worship their own religion, speak their own language, listen to their own music, and eat their own food? Why can't we be Mexican the same as the Irish, the Italians, the Polish, or the French? Are we so threatening that we must be constantly under attack?

My experience in the military went by likes a flash. It felt as if it was only yesterday that I was walking the Hermiston High School track and then circled the football field, a place where I found protection from the aggressive nature of the world outside of my insulated environment. Whoever invented the game of football must have had some anger issues and decided that this game would be a perfect cover to disguise what was hidden just under the surface of my true emotions. For me, football was a perfect solution that allowed me to release the tensions that I internalized, allowing them to boil over when anything contradicted my expectations.

Two years after I joined the military, I returned home as a different person with a different sense of myself and of what my next few years would look like. The Army provided me with an invaluable experience of being exposed to the diversity of humanity, allowing me to discover my appreciation for the uniqueness of our small world. Curiosity became the door to knowledge about others, where they come from, and the different values and perspectives that people carry with them that were not much different than the ones I was taught.

Military service and my early years of traveling across the western part of the United States, living in labor camps or small rural agricultural communities while growing up surrounded by Anglo kids prepared me for the challenges that I would face as I expanded my vision. The lessons I had learned as a boy became more evident. The notion that my ancestors had of leaving the place of origin and going out to accumulate knowledge and learn from others to better understand the new beginning became a driving force for how I wanted to approach life.

Now that I was back, I had to figure out how to succeed in college. Armed with an early out from the Army, I enrolled at Blue Mountain Community College with an understanding that my goal was to do well and go from there to the University of Oregon for a degree in art education. My obstacle was to raise my low level of academic achievement in high school. Community college was the answer, so I returned to BMCC near Hermiston, not because I couldn't afford to go anywhere else but because I couldn't get into any other school. After all, my grade point average out of high school was a 2.1, not something to be proud of but good enough to graduate from high school.

If Mr. Wilson had been there on enrollment day at BMCC, he would have heard a young angry Chicano scream, "Eat shit, Mr. Wilson! Neither you nor your buddies will stop me. I will return to let you know what someone who refuses to listen to your shit can accomplish."

My vision had been chiseled into my spirit; anger of the past into passion for success would serve as my driving force, focused on proving that no one but me had the power to decide what my destiny would be. From my first day of classes, it was clear I was ready to be there, that my spirit was hungry to learn new things that would allow me to think beyond my reality. As new knowledge was thrown in my direction and dumped into my mind, it became easier to understand where things fit, at least through the eyes of a college student who had never been a part of the mainstream. My sense of how things should be was not necessarily consistent with mainstream thinking. I was different, and I came from a different part of the world.

There was no confusion for me that various parts of the country were in turmoil over things that were not so obvious to the students sheltered at BMCC. Most students on campus had not experienced other parts of the country with the extreme poverty that had developed since the expansion beyond the early villages of the country's beginnings. It was not hard to understand why there was a civil rights movement taking place or why there was an activist fringe in opposition to the war in Vietnam. Dissatisfaction was everywhere, and nothing remained sacred. What had been a part of the past was a target for challenge and, eventually, for change. Rebellion was so rampant that even those foundations, such as a strong nuclear family that had worked for centuries, were open to challenge and could eventually change forever. It seemed as if somewhere in the advancement of a nation, the people had lost touch with each other and could no longer remember what it took to be a community.

The turmoil that America was experiencing became even

more transparent to me through my experience in the military. The exposure to a diversity of races, cultures, and subcultures produced an unintended education that caused me to question the substance that drives this nation. Experiential education planted the seed of caution, causing me to question if life, liberty, and the pursuit of happiness were guaranteed to everyone. How could we have a country that could send young soldiers across the planet to fight for other people's democracy, liberty, and human rights to the point of sacrificing 56,000 young lives with hundreds of thousands changed forever in war?

While young African American and Mexican American men and women were fighting for others, there was no one there to protect their families from racism, shootings, or lynchings. How was it possible to have human beings lynched in the South and a Chicano in New Mexico shot at a gas station for trying to get water for a car that overheated? Why were we willing to tolerate farm workers living in third-world conditions, working for slave wages, living in shacks with no plumbing, and using outhouses and community showers without any concern as to how to improve conditions and ensure that the farmworkers' children would not have to continue to live this way?

The more I learned, the more the inequities began to reveal themselves, the angrier I became. Where is the government that calls us to serve when we are needed, and we go without question? Why do we go? Because we love this nation in spite of the fact that it has ignored our communities for decades. If the threat to democracy was taking place in Korea, Vietnam, or Latin America, we would intervene because it is the righteous thing to do, the human thing to do. Hey! People are starving to death over there. But what shall we do for the starving people over here?

***

Success as a college student came easy because of my

community college experience. Starting at a small college was a good decision for me, especially when the ties of dependency to the Army had not yet been broken. My transition back to the world went from being released in Germany to Fort Dix, New Jersey, then taking a bus across the country to Hermiston. I arrived on a Sunday and walked the four miles to our home to find out that my family no longer lived there. To my surprise, my family had moved from Oregon back to southern Texas along the Mexico border without letting me know. When I finally reached my father and asked him why he hadn't told me, his immediate reply was, "You didn't write."

It took a bit, but I began to realize that many other people in this community had been a big part of my life. I also learned that my brother Gerardo had moved to a town only twenty miles away.

The following Monday, the changes really started. I enrolled at BMCC. And I was on my own. Time to think about finding my own place to live and buy clothes with more than just Army green. While standing in line waiting to register for classes, thoughts of being isolated engulfed me, and I had another realization: building relationships and making friends was not something we had to learn in the Army. Friends were established out of necessity with the knowledge that we might never see each other again once we left that duty station. They were friendships forged out of the need to have people who would watch your back and protect you from the diverse groups that formed at each base that sometimes fought each other like the gangs in the cities. Here in line, instead of seeing the brotherhood handshake that was an acknowledgment of membership and belonging, there were only cowboy boots, big hats, the circular imprint of a can of Skoal on the back pocket of Wrangler jeans, and those snow-covered mountains that had driven me away the last time.

Almost two years had passed, yet things were still the same. Some of the same students were still attending classes, not knowing what their major would be, and their most difficult decision was how many credits to take and what to focus on.

My journey had taken me full circle, returning as a different individual, seeing the world with different eyes. Inside, my heart had grown stronger with the pain but less tolerant of the injustice. Like many other young people, what had been accepted in the past was no longer acceptable for the future. Full circle, and the journey points to the books and education, the time to begin the work of learning why the conflict inside of me had no answers. Some of my friends chose another path, the path of violent protest, that path of action without knowledge. Only one choice was available to me, and that was to understand what my enemy was and fight it with the strongest weapon: knowledge.

CHAPTER 17
Higher Learning

No estudio por saber más, sino poor ignorar menos.
(I don't study to know more, but to ignore less.)
~ Dicho

With a sense of curiosity, a focus on the future, and a ferocious appetite to learn as much as possible, my formal education became a reality. It was no longer the tale of what could or would be. Launched at the community college, it transported me on my journey and beyond those snow-covered mountains. Even though it had been almost two years, the classes were being taught by the same professors. A couple of them asked why they had not seen me around. God, is it so easy to dismiss people that we can lose track of whether they have been in town or off in some other country wearing a uniform? After all, it wasn't as if it were a huge city, where missing someone for two years would be out of the ordinary. It was a town of 17,000 people. Just enough to have a low profile for a while but not big enough to go unnoticed for too long. It didn't matter whether anyone knew. What mattered was that a new path was waiting to take me on a new journey. Only, this time the journey would go beyond the limits of return.

Classes began and it seemed easier than my memory recalled from my short stay two years before. Initially, I took oil painting, art appreciation, and the basics needed for a degree. Nothing was challenging, but it was just enough to carry a full load so I could qualify for the GI Bill. To my surprise, the load seemed easy, and by the end of the quarter and a 3.6 GPA, I knew that the face in the mirror had changed. Who was this person who could get these kinds of grades with ease when the same person had been lucky to graduate from high school? Maybe that old curandera had put a spell on me?

Blue Mountain was only in the cards for a year until my transfer to the University of Oregon in Eugene. While on campus I got exposed to many activist student groups that were concerned with the issues on the environment, social justice, affordable housing and the ones that caught my attention were the groups involved with farm workers. I heard many stories of Chicano brothers and sisters involved in the United Farm Worker (UFW) movement. Being the only Chicano at Blue Mountain, it was hard to find anyone to relate to my interest in the UFW. The farmworker families that lived in the area had been in the region for four or five generations, and they were farmers themselves or part of the general labor force. The only exceptions were the few Indians who attended the college from the Umatilla or the Yakima reservations. My buddy Ben could have been there with me, but the courts had given him the choice of jail or the Army. Ben was still in the war somewhere, and no one had heard from him, but there was never a question as to whether he would return. He was Sioux and destined for other trials.

Nine months after my arrival home, the U of O accepted me into the School of Education starting in September. Only the summer was left to think about what would come next. I spent it working in the fields with my family, making some extra cash for the fall. It was also useful in reminding me of what we faced as migrant farm workers. It solidified the resolve in my mind that success was the only choice to have options in the future.

Working the summer before going to the big university brought home the love that had been missing since high school graduation. Everyone was there—Tias Rico, Lupe, and Concha. Tios Camote (Francisco), La Coneja (Andres, the rabbit),

Geronimo, and Jose. When I finally caught up with them, they were in Othello, Washington, picking potatoes. And so, my work began. We were settled in a small labor camp just outside of town. Nothing had changed: we were always just outside of town, just far away enough to be invisible, far enough away to become "those people," and never a part of any community. Somehow, it didn't matter now because for the first time in years, love engulfed every part of my spirit.

The work that summer was as hard as any memory could conjure. The summer sun was as brilliant and hot as ever, with the dust blowing in my eyes and caking the rims of my lips, but there was always laughing and joking. For a time, the workers' attention was on me because of my absence for the last couple of years. They would break out in an orchestra of laughter when I told them of my plan for attending the university. "Those Anglos won't let you in there," they yelled as they picked the spuds. "Hell, where will you get the money? You are not making any more than we are, and we can barely feed ourselves."

If the truth had been known, my fears would have been the same as theirs. They had just been hidden to keep me from losing courage. Laughter continued throughout the summer, a spirit of joy glazed with the knowledge that there would be another time and another place. Things would not always be as they are, and our time was near. God would make sure that we were provided for. "Don't worry about things you can't control," Tia Rico would always remind me, "God will guide you."

Summer finally ended, and it stirred up the same melancholy from my youth, as if I was walking away from someone I loved. There seemed to be many warm memories around the ritual of working the land as our ancestors did in the sacred valley of Mexico before we were forced to scatter to the ends of the earth. It was painful to think about my next journey because of the implications it might have on my relationship with my family. For the first time, I had a premonition that pulled at me with a gnawing instinct that returning to these familiar surroundings would change with this next journey. And then there was the choice of deciding whether this is what was intended for me and whether the next step was necessary to make things better, if not for my family, at least for people in my community. There was no decision to be made. The decision had been made long before.

My career as a student was as an activist. Like a magnet drawing discarded iron shavings closer together to create a more valuable piece of steel, my attention was immediately drawn to those radical and beautiful people of color. Most of us came from similar communities, simply diverse cultures, and settings. Our common bond was one of ending the exploitation of the workers and fighting for the freedoms that America had promised us. We collaborated with each other: the Indians of the Pine Ridge (Ben's old home), the African Americans on busing, and the Chicanos on farm worker issues. We were brothers and sisters in a cause, not just because. Exploitation and oppression were our enemy, and equity with equality was our agenda. Politics entered my sphere of knowledge and with it came the various political philosophies that had influenced entire nations in the past.

It became a time when young mestizo warriors had awakened with the consciousness that we had been here before the Pilgrims and the Spaniards. We were still here with our wisdom of the prophecy predicting the recovery of the ancient lands and the fact that time would be our witness. Young warriors were returning from the military with a renewed vigor, willing to fight and die for the opportunity to have choices in life's decisions. To fight for the ability to choose to go to law school or medical school or become a mechanic, gardener, or laborer. It was a time of struggle for human dignity. My only choice was to further my education in the mainstream system and learn as much as possible to combat the inequities my eyes had seen as a child.

I thirsted for the knowledge that would help me fight the oppression of poverty that has haunted my ancestors for centuries as they wandered throughout this continent.

Perhaps learning more would provide the key that would unlock the mystery of Aztlán. The same priests who buried the scrolls of knowledge to keep them from the Spaniards were the ones who asked the old ones to wander the earth in search of the truth. Knowledge was to be gained, obtained, and protected. It was also a tool guiding people through their daily lives.

Early campfire lessons as a young migrant farm worker taught me that my ancestors were everything that a flourishing civilization demanded. My father knew that critical to my spirit was knowing my roots and understanding the substance that made me a person. His careful reinforcement of our ancestral history was the wall that kept the insecurity and the weakness of a lost identity away from the spirit that guided my soul. He was cautious to provide me with enough ancestral knowledge to provide me with an intense sense of pride and create a positive self-image. It gave me a vision of how to continue the legacy of the ancient people that brought us to this earth.

There were signs of their presence everywhere: in art, architecture, mathematics, astrology, and in writings of ancient myths. My hunger for an education came from the need to learn more about who we are and to fight as if they fought for nothing but a simple truth.

I had lived most of my life in America, exposed to a mainstream culture that had no knowledge of the place of our origin and our accomplishments, and respected our language even less. It became important to learn what Americans knew. My challenge was to learn the American ways, master English, and take part in social activities in a way that would be acceptable without giving up the value of my beginning. How was I to keep my self-identity in a world that is intolerant of people who are different but believe to the point of worship that there is room for individuals? How could you be an individual and not be different from everyone else?

If individuals do exist in this great nation, then why can't people who are different in language and culture be accepted as readily as the individual? It seems that an individual fits well into this society if that individual is White and of similar religious beliefs and similar social values. So much for the individual and the acceptance of differences. My only choice was to learn how to be competitive in this world while holding on to my world in private. There could be no other way because being white is not an option. Spanish will always be my first language and Indian blood will always run through my veins.

Life brought challenges to my door, the greatest of which was how to control my anger at what was happening to communities throughout the nation and in my life.

Where Are You, God?

Wiping tears, a fragile face smiles,

Choking on a thick fog of hatred.

He was always there,

A noble knight on guard.

Constancy, consistency, consumed by an

Impatience of a busy world.

Need to get to the store to buy a loaf of bread,

Don't forget the milk.

For God's sake, don't forget the paper.

Oh, and pick up the dry cleaning.

One of the vehicles needs an oil change.

Aggravation drives the moment, which car?

Disgust surrounds the landscape.

Excuse me, but I am too busy.

Shit!

What happened to that man who used to sit on the corner?

He was here yesterday.

Why don't they just get a job?

Can't they work like everyone else?

They make everyone nervous.

Standing in the same place sixteen hours a day.

Hey, weren't they here yesterday?

Don't they ever leave?

Where is their family, their children?

Is he here during the holidays?

God!

He doesn't live here, does he?

Did he move, or did someone make him move?

A light blue fog hugging the soil of souls,

Scent of burning pine,

Sounds of sizzling pitch,

Nostrils flare, stinging of smoke.

Clothes carry the invader.

Beyond its boundary, invading your space.

In the distance, children's laughter pursuing happiness,

Tractors building earth clouds from parched soil,

A straight white line pushing a silver plane to paradise.

A lifetime of struggling with enough heartbreak for several lives can push anyone to question the values that support their existence. How long does it take to break out of the situation of despair that grows heavy on a young heart? Despair that brings with it anger and impatience. There seems to be no way out. We were meant to live a life of challenge, wandering the earth until the time for the chosen generation to rise and assume their New World role in peace and harmony. All that was needed would be to find a way to break through, to be able to access the opportunities available to others that allow them to move back and forth through the social and economic wall keeping our people from the choices of a better life. The only way out seemed to be to find a shortcut to accommodate that place where people could live in nice homes with showers, toilets, running water, and paved streets leading to other beautiful homes. Why wait when there were many different ways to access affluence? Some of my new friends from the university seemed to find ways to make quick money and become part of the middle class. Maybe they were always middle class and only seemed like me when they were college students.

CHAPTER 18
The Shortcut Becomes the Goal

La primera obligación de todo ser humano es ser feliz,
la segunda es hacer efliz a los demas.
(The first obligation of every human being is to be
happy; the second is to make others happy.)
~ Dicho

At some point, I lost my sense of direction and changed my focus from hard work to looking for an easier way to make more money. The dream was almost lost when I gave way to the weakness of expedience and the path of least resistance to easy answers. Always seeking the quickest way of achieving the vision of success can easily overwhelm you until the shortcut becomes the goal. It is easy to see what it could be, but just as easy to lose the drive to get there. Allowing yourself to be consumed by greed will prevent you from conceptualizing your destination. Without a destination, there is no journey.

During my time of confusion, greed, and recklessness, the importance of pursuing knowledge with a sense of the past had no place to go. Overindulgence in what seemed pleasure pushed me further from family, home, deliverance from poverty, and the wealth of knowledge to find a place in history. This period, even though it had only been a speck of time in the evolution of who I had become, could destroy generations of preparation for the journey to eventually return to the unknown destination. The cliff-walking with the law, drugs, and violence would have sabotaged my pursuit to become someone of substance and knowledge.

Anger was driving me on a collision course with evil—the type of evil my tias used to tell me stories about, like the man who had been walking along the railroad track after a night of drinking and chasing whores in a place that everyone knew as the place down under. The young men called it "Boys' Town." As the story went, this man spent all his weekly wages drinking and taking a couple of women for the right price; at least, it was the right price for Pedro after eight or ten beers. Finally, after his lust was satiated and there was no more room for any more alcohol, Pedro decided to walk home. He chose to take the shortcut along the railroad tracks.

Just as he got away from the lights of town and the memory of his evening's activities began to slip from his mind, Pedro noticed a small black cat walking parallel to him but at a distance—close enough to be noticed but yet far enough so as not to be in any danger from human touch and aloof enough to ignore all of Pedro's calls. The cat followed him for at least a mile ignoring all of Pedro's attempts to befriend him. As the lights of the town began to disappear totally, Pedro noticed that the cat began to glow a bright red orange. Suddenly, the cat seemed to stumble. As it fell forward, it appeared to curl up and roll into a ball the color of fire.

Pedro could not believe his eyes and just as he began to get more curious, the cat rolled slowly toward him. As Pedro stepped back, fearing the cat, it began to roll faster, causing Pedro to move back again. Pedro found himself turning in the opposite direction and stepping into the night with every bit of light sucked from the sky and only the glowing fire that was pursuing him. By now, he was running at full speed as fast as his heart and legs could manage with only one thought, and that was to get to the comfort and safety of his home, where he would find his wife and children.

Pedro finally made it home and barely escaped being consumed by the fiery cat. God must have been with him that evening, or at least he thought so. That evening was the last time Pedro went to the place down under. His fear of what happened was too great, and he became extremely sick after that evening. Pedro died a few weeks later in his own bed with a fiery red glow over his body as he lay there for the mourners.

Like Pedro, the early lessons passed on to me by my tias had begun to slip from my memory. I was close to giving up the struggle to succeed by allowing myself to believe that money and temporary pleasure were the way out of the anger I felt in knowing that my family was poor and there was nothing that could be done about it.

Poverty alone did not create the anger beneath the smile and laughter that everyone could see in me. My anger grew from the knowledge that people from my community, including my immediate family, were working in the fields for minimal wages from dawn to dusk seven days a week. And they often worked without pay until the entire harvests were completed, only to have a coyote (labor contractor) take a percentage of the wages. A percentage of the pay was for the privilege of being able to work on the farm, or at least that was the logic of the coyote.

It should not be a great surprise to find violent anger in the children of a generation when their culture, heritage, and the essence of their being are degraded at every turn. It became amazingly easy to believe in money and what it could do for me immediately, never recognizing the heavy burden it would have on my soul. Like Pedro, it was too late when I realized the ultimate price for artificial success. Success disguised by pleasures created by drugs, alcohol, quick money, and the easy life meant giving up the essence of what was passed on to me by my ancestors. I was at risk of losing the values of my Yucatan Indian family. They left their homeland in search of greater knowledge and a better way of life for what could be gained. The future offered shelter and enough food to eat, and we could become wiser human beings. Those values allowed me to survive and overcome life choices that challenged me.

No logical reason existed to explain why anyone would abandon the spirit and purpose of the soul for the temporary satisfaction found in a bottle or a quick snort of a white powder. Drinking the liquid has the effect of changing a charitable human being into someone who could knife another person or break a beer bottle over their face, scaring them for life. Reflecting on those lost years when I walked a fine line between sanity and insanity, I can see that I was constantly beyond the legal boundaries that would have taken me straight to prison.

I would have been the ideal candidate for La Llorona's search for people like me who have forgotten the teachings, the old ways of how we are to be with each other, especially the forgotten lessons of respect for those around you but especially respect for yourself. My direction had been blurred from the outside and La Llorona wanted to bring me back. Every time my mind began to dance with the notion of artificial success, my thoughts drifted to the thought of La Llorona chasing my Tio Camote, and I feared it would happen to me. La Llorna searches the world to save its lost children from ancient Aztlán.

Even in reflection, it is difficult to explain why I would allow myself to enter a world of evil, dominated by little bags of white powder and alcohol. The lost years of money, drugs, alcohol, and irresponsibility led to a life without clarity of purpose or direction. My family helped me come back to the life they raised me to live. The memories of the early lessons of love, compassion for other human beings, the difference between right and wrong, and the strength of the family would guide me back to a path of purpose and direction. They provided me with the road map that led me to the next turning point.

The values I gained in the labor camps, all the love and support that I received growing up, and the sense of shame if they knew that gave in to the weaknesses of ordinary people, helped me shift. After all, they thought I was special, and we came from a world of pyramid builders, poets, astronomers, and explorers, and now I was giving this up for $8,000 a month and all the coke I could snort. Not much of a tradeoff when I was coming from a place of origin.

The different paths I chose in getting to where I am today were not always the right paths. Decisions of where to go next, whether to risk the security of where I was or to take a path that had no map to guide me faced me head-on when I least expected them. I was guilty of living a life that went contrary to my ancestors. The sentinels of the pyramids would never accept me back into the community if I were poisoned by the foreign and evil direction I had chosen from anger. My only guidance has been the gift of knowing that I need to question my acts and decide whether it is the right or wrong thing to do. Of course, there were times in my youth when I deliberately chose to do the wrong thing, defying the sense of right and wrong for immediate pleasures or rewards.

After many years of giving in to the weakness of immediate pleasure, I came to realize there was always a price to pay and that I never got away with anything. The greatest loss of all was the loss of time and what I could have done by just making the choices I knew were right. I have come to learn that there are no shortcuts to success or instant pleasures that are long-lasting.

Time gives everyone the gift of wisdom, which allows us to see more clearly. It provides us with transparency to see the effects of our decisions of the past. While I have been guilty of wasting the treasure of time, my guilt was always haunted by the thought of what my family would say if I let go altogether and chose to lose myself in unmapped territory on a voyage that did not allow a return passage.

I was guilty of giving in to seven years of anger that had built up over my life with no way to escape in a safe and controlled manner. Just as I found myself graduating from undergraduate school and looking forward to beginning my career, I was stopped at a crossroads. My dilemma was to decide between working for the people who needed my service in support of young people or making money. At the time, the decision seemed simple. The choices were to continue working in a Head Start program with young children and their families, families interested in getting an early start for their children, and to continue working at a boy's ranch with young men who had had minor run-ins with the law or go to Alaska to work on the pipeline and get rich.

Deciding did not take much consideration for someone who had grown up in poverty and spent most of his life trying to break out. The choice was to go to Alaska and get rich. After all, getting out of poverty had always been my goal.

The temptation of making bundles of money working on the pipeline and the news accounts on the television of union workers making thousands of dollars a month without having to pay for living expenses became my answer. I could go to Alaska and get rich. Like an unfinished sentence, which was as far as I got. Choices and simple decisions are not always as simple as they seem.

Alaska was never part of my vision or plan for myself. The decision to go to Alaska came from an overwhelming urge that I believe was genetic, having come from a mixed DNA bloodline of Mexica Indian blood of Azted, Mayan, Inca, and Spanish, all of which had a history of wandering in search of a place. Since my early twenties, I have always felt this, knawing in the back of my mind that it constantly pushed me to go find out what was beyond the horizon. My conclusion was that I had wander lust, but now that I am older, I have come to realize that it was my need to search for our place of origin. Alaska was a place of white surrounded by mountains, a place of wonderment that was home to many ancient tribes and I got to know and understand some of the Indigenous people I met. It was common for me to find myself thinking they looked like someone from home. We had so many common features I began to question if there could be some connection.

For me, Alaska was also a place of adventure and

exploration. My decision to quit the job I was doing with a county HeadStart program, abandoned everything I had known and head north with a call from some college friends who had grown up in Alaska and found themselves working on the Alaska pipeline that had involved over seventy thousand people from all over the world to build. I had only worked for the HeadStart for a school year when I received a call from the O'Donnell brothers, there were four of them and each with a separate talent all with higher-than-average intelligence.

It was an early Sunday morning when I received a call from John, the brother and poet writer who was second in line. They were all at the Fairbanks bar, a place that had two bars, one in reserve that could open so the one that had been open all night could be cleaned. The call came in in the early morning when the brothers were switching bars after a night of who knows what. John called to tell me that I should go to Alaska and join them and that I could make a lot of money. It was great to hear from my friends but the idea of going to Alaska to make a lot of money did not motivate me. Yes, it piqued my interest, but I was not ready to make that move. There was decent work to be done where I was.

I continued working at HeadStart and struggling with my low salary while reminded by my daily struggle to make ends meet that I had grown up in poverty and getting an education was going to be my way out. It became clear to me that the path I was on would only keep me in a state of poverty but only at a higher level. There are many levels of poverty and even though I had entered the professional ranks, I was still poor. The second time John called to tell me there were a lot of jobs and they could help get on the pipeline I decided to jump into the pond headfirst. I said yes and they told me that Luke, another friend of ours, was going up as well and Luke and I decided to drive my VW bug to Alaska to go work on the pipeline.

Having spent my youth traveling across the country with my family as a migrant worker I knew that I would need to service the VW. Well as I began to learn of the conditions that we would encounter on the drive north, I quickly found out that driving the Alcan Highway would require carrying chains because even though it was spring there would be snow and frozen roads most of the way and there would be almost thirteen hundred miles of gravel. I would need to get plastic covers for my headlights, chains, battery warmer, and gas heater. Even though it was early spring, there would be places that could still hit thirty degrees below zero.

Our trip began in Oregon with some of the best Mexican weed we could find and special mushrooms that could make any environment appear glorious. Oh my god, what a beautiful place to have mushrooms. What we did not consider was the Canadian checkpoint where they stopped us because we looked suspicious. Of course, we looked suspicious, with long hair, overgrown beards, and eyes dilated the size of the moon. Who wouldn't pull us over? What was surprising was that they went through everything in the car, including removing the carpet from the floor board. How they never found what we were carrying, I will never know.

After our two-hour ordeal, we were on our way. The drive greeted us with a couple of snowstorms, ice, gigantic potholes, and endless miles of beautiful scenery and wildlife. We were on the drive of a lifetime that did not require any type of stimulant. Nature and wildlife provided all of that in the most organic way. The trip through Oregon, Washington, and western Canada, the Yukon territory, was indescribable and can only be shared successfully in person. It was the type of trip that reminded me how small I was in the scheme of the universe. It was the first time that I began to understand the relationship my elders had with the environment they lived in and how we took from it and that we must return something and only take what we need.

Arriving in Fairbanks, it felt like driving into a frontier town exuberant with uncontrolled celebration; driving into town at ten in the morning, the bars were overflowing with people actively celebrating the moment. Instantly, I felt a surge of nervousness; it seemed like a place with no structure, and I wondered how the work gets done. How can these people be building a pipeline? Pulling into my friends' house there were guys in the yard drinking and wrestling in the mud that should have been a lawn. They were at the end of a three-day celebration of coming down from the slope, which meant that they had spent at least three months north of Fairbanks in isolated camps that could only be reached by plane in the most remote camps and by pipeline trucks in the camps that were within the artic circle. After three days of celebration and spending most of their earnings for the three months on the slope some would go to their homes in the lower forty-eight.

Things began to quiet down that evening, and I was given a spot to sleep in the corner of the basement. A couple of days went by, and the haze from the previous days of partying had worn off. My friends decided it was time to go out again. This time, I went with them, and it turned out to be an experience that could not exist anywhere else. The first thing I noticed was that there were no rules, and inhibitions were nonexistent. While people were making a lot of money, there appeared no sense of the value of what they had earned and no sense of the future. It was the first time that I saw behavior that had no consideration for the future.

Reckless and unencumbered partying wasn't anything that resembled a conscience; it was not something I had allowed myself to feel, but it was the spirit in this isolated world of plenty. It was not long before I allowed myself to let go and join with reckless abandon, finding that this feeling was frightening in that it felt that you could go so far that you might not be able to find your way back. After a month of doing nothing but partying, I finally told my friend John that I needed to start working. He told me that all the jobs were union jobs, and I had to join the union, and that there were hundreds of people on the list waiting to get out.

In his next breath, he said, "I know a guy that we can talk to that can help you. I will set up a meeting so you can let him know you want to work." Of course, I immediately agreed. The plan was to go to the airport bar and wait for the union guy to show up and John would let me know when to go to his table to introduce myself. After an hour or so of drinking John leaned over to let me know the guy was here and that he was ready to introduce me. He went on to tell me that all I had to do was to let him know I was looking for a job on the slope and when he (John) gave me the high sign to hand him the five hundred dollars that he gave me. The introduction went as planned and the union person asked me, "So you are looking for a job on the slop?"

I answered yes, and as I did, John nudged my leg to let me know it was time to hand him the money under the table. Nothing else was said, and the next thing I heard was, "You need to be at the airport at 6 a.m. and catch the flight to Cold Foot Camp."

The next thing I knew, I was on the slope in the middle of the Brooks Range ready to go to work. I landed in Cold Foot and was assigned a trailer with another person. I went there to drop my things, and as I started to walk down the stairs, I spotted the most beautiful German shepherd I had ever seen, and as I was coaxing him to come to me, I realized that there were no pets in the camp that far north. And like they say in Boston, dawn came to Marble Head, and I realized that this was not someone's pet but a large wolf. This was my introduction to the wildness of where I was. The camp was constantly visited by wolves, black bears, brown bears, badgers, and other wildlife that lived there long before our presence.

Life on the slope was fast, wild, and crazy, laced with an unpredictability that occurs when you put people together from all over the world looking for adventure and fortune. Cold Foot, at the height of construction, was a camp for 850 people with only eight women. I cannot imagine the difficulty that the women had to deal with.

My first boss in camp had just been released from a prison in Illinois where he had been imprisoned for manslaughter, and it wasn't long before I found out firsthand that it was his temper that landed him a prison sentence as he chased someone through the dining room with a knife in his hand. We had to jump him to stop him and convince him to cool down. My roommate was on work release from a federal prison in Washington. When I got the courage to ask what he did to go to prison, he told me it was for dealing cocaine. He said he was one of the biggest dealers on the West Coast when he got caught. For me, that was a head-scratcher; he was here making over one hundred thousand dollars a year going into his bank account until he fulfilled his prison sentence. So, he was on work release, reporting periodically to the prison when he had to take time off, and he was accumulating in his bank account over a hundred thousand dollars a year. Who says crime doesn't pay?

Life in the camps was littered with characters with human flaws that were as diverse as the population that was building the pipeline. There were laborers, teamsters, welders, pipeline, and culinary workers. You name it, and the skill or craft was working on the pipeline. Life on the pipeline was filled by living today as it was going to be that last day with alcohol, drugs, guns, and gambling everywhere you looked, all of which were prohibited in camp. It was a life that was moving so fast that I knew if I stayed for a prolonged period, my life would be cut short. I remember drinking with a friend of mine who was paralyzed from the waist down, and he was sitting on a five-gallon can that appeared as if it had been used for flour or lard, he looked at me as he finished his shot and asked me if I wanted to do some coke. I said yes just because I didn't want to be a pussy.

He grabbed his braces, propped himself up, leaned against the table and popped the lid on the can where I saw the entire can was full of coke. It was then that I knew that I did not belong, otherwise I would either end up in prison or dead.

My wanderlust began to haunt me once more, only this time it was not for a place but a purpose. I knew that I had moved away from everything I had been taught and could only think of the shame I would bring my elders if I ended up killing myself with drugs or alcohol and, worse yet, ended up in prison. There could be no forgiveness for such reckless behavior. After three years of being lost in a fog, I found myself trying to find my back to the person I used to know.

CHAPTER 19
A New Race

We must use our lives to make the world a better place to live, not just to acquire things. That is what we are put on the earth for.
~ Dolores Huerta

Growing up as a seasonal farmworker, I experienced life in various parts of the country. I was forced at an early age to consider where I fit in. As my life experiences expanded and my exposure to different regions of the county became personal adventures, I began to see a much larger community than the place we came from in southern Mexico. Life through my expanded lens showed me different lifestyles and brought me closer to an understanding of what the elders meant when they prophesized that we would go out into the world, accumulate new knowledge, and experience new ways of life that would shape our people into a new race. Beyond the melding of multiple cultures and races as a people, we accumulated cultural knowledge that would lead us to a diverse cultural destiny. We would become a new people, a blended humanity.

I gradually learned that many groups of people, like mine, came from ancient cultures and had a history that contained stories of what they would become in the future. More importantly, I noticed that, as people, we all have some common needs and desires.

People want to live in hope that they can thrive in a world that acknowledges their humanity with respect, that their families will be safe, that their children will have opportunities to become more knowledgeable than the elders, and that we can live in a place that supports our needs. As I've gotten older, I've internalized that we all have the capacity for love.

While I have gained a better understanding of the good that is possible, I have questions that still have no answers and that constantly surface across our different communities. What is it that creates a division between communities and pits one group over another? Why should some people have while others have not, and the have-nots do the work to support the haves, who get wealthy off the sweat of men, women, and children who have no voice?

Some believe that our system of government and the economy drive our livelihood to run more smoothly when those who produce wealth are silent. All over this country, angry eyes are staring out of Brown and Black faces. People of color everywhere are experiencing attacks on their existence.

I don't understand where the hatred comes from. How can human beings spend so much time hating others they don't even know? Where is it written that we should live in separate parts of town, shop at different stores, eat at different restaurants, and only marry within groups? It seems unnatural that anyone could function to their full ability if they are constantly having to think of where they can or cannot go and to whom they can or cannot talk to or marry. Why should I have to worry about where I drink water or watch a movie?

Life as a migrant farm worker exposed me to many who owned that hatred, which prompted them to shout obscenities at us without knowing who we were. My early travels with my family to work on farms in California, Oregon, Washington, and Utah were my daily reminders of my position in this society. Of course, not all Latinos chose to do what they were supposed to do or took their assigned place in society's structured plan. Some of us choose to follow our destinies. I recall my father quoting Emiliano Zapata: "It is better to die on my feet than to live on my knees." This has stayed with me. I was one of those Mexican kids who chose to raise my head and ask why. I chose to say no! I will not live this way any longer.

Of course, as a young man, I did not know exactly how I would live or even what I would do, but I knew I had to fight for my existence. Constant racial conflict creates a person who is in a continuous state of alertness in public places to avoid confrontation with people who whisper obscenities as they pass and would celebrate if they enticed a person of color to respond to their vulgarities. After all, a response from a young Mejicano would only bring the police and guess who would go to jail. Now these feelings of hatred and racism are not new, but they have been recently renewed and allowed to be shown in public.

Sophisticated racism in this country has evolved into an art form, an evolution that supports the economic and social status quo as well as the physical separation of people who could grow and learn from each other. Filtered education has become a tool to continue discriminatory practices that are overt and in the past and were skewed through history lessons, public policy, and the very government put in place to protect them. New diversions have been created, such as discrimination of the majority against the majority, creating chaos that makes it difficult to distinguish which communities are experiencing the greatest losses. Recently we have seen separate groups from the majority populations pitted against one another over perceived religious requirements or access to the larger economic opportunities.

On reflection, I have gone through many stages in my life with specific and decisive moments where small decisions led to major changes, hurling me into a direction that shifted and then formed my destiny. At other times, just the thought of change, action, and thought of that change melted into one destiny, like a glacier back to the sea after its voyage around the world. I have never been clear which was the more powerful, my subtle actions or the power of spontaneous thought. Does a person have the ability to visualize themselves in another setting and project themselves there? Can they better their lives through visualization, or is acting the key to success? Through my life of constant change, I have concluded that faith, vision, and action are all necessary elements to achieving a person's goal. My goal has been to break out of poverty and help others break through the same barrier.

During the many days and years, I've spent trying to sort this out, I began to understand the mystery of that confusion. Who have I become, and when did I become that being? I cannot remember when the changes occurred or when the thought occurred. There are no specific dates to look back on to say that is when I became Victor. It has been a transition of experiences and the influences of many people. And it has been a transition of generations through culture and ancestors who left behind accumulated secrets. Do I act like my father, grandfather, or great-grandmother? Or am I the conglomeration of the past and the creation of a history for the future?

There have been multiple times in my life that this realization struck, this brief history in my mind. These specific unanswered questions cause turmoil, anger, and the relentless push to continue moving forward. My sense of Identity I owe to my father, Victoriano Escobar Vasquez, who gave me the gifts that allowed me to dream without boundaries, to know who I was, and never give in to the pressures of those who want me to be someone else. A dreamer I became, and my only true fear is that I stop dreaming or miss an opportunity.

I have never found the beginning of my unanswered questions. Many young Mexican Americans have grown up with more questions than answers. They have learned that calling themselves Mexican can be interpreted that they are illegal or undocumented. To call themselves American can mean that they are Tio Tacos (Uncle Toms), a person who has shunned their Latino culture. Children sit and wait patiently and observe as we argue amongst ourselves and ask what we should call ourselves. I have been called Meskin, Mexican, greaser, wetback, Hispanic, and now Latinx. No one has ever asked us what we want to be called.

An acquaintance of mine from my hometown once told me, "Don't call me Chicano, pendejo. That is an insult to all Hispanics."

As I looked him straight in the eye with a fiery glare from my oval obsidian eyes inherited from my ancestors, I shot back, "Who's panic? Are you? His—Panic? I am no one's panic." Hispanic is not even a word. It's a term the federal government made up to be able to count the diverse Latinos who were living in the U.S. This man had no idea who he really was or any sense of his heritage.

Hispanic is not from our language or anything that we choose to call ourselves. This name was given to us for the 1980 census so the Anglos could count us. I think this is the first time that they realized that we came in all colors as well because during that census we had to distinguish between Black and non-White Hispanics.

"Pendejo," I shot back, "I am a Chicano, and I chose to call myself that because of my political interest and because of my Mexican cultural heritage. After all, we have become the beings that we are because of ethnicity and culture and not race. A person can only be defined by the group of people that raises them. I was raised by Mexicans with Indian blood and have always been proud of it."

How many children ask themselves, *what is my name? Is it José, or is it Joe? My parents call me José, yet my schoolteacher and classmates call me Joe. When did my name go through that transition? Who granted permission for it to change? Is my new legal name legal?* This is why I am a Chicano por La Causa, and that, pendejo, is why your name Phillipe became Philip and why you can be Hispanic. I have no idea who that guy is anymore. I do know that he is working for the sheriff, undercover he says, and turns in people from the community because it makes him feel important.

As a child growing up in Mexican culture and thrown into the American Anglo culture in school, I have memories of children playing, running around in circles, chanting playful words but not understanding what those words meant. How can a child go through childhood without learning nursery rhymes or learning those games that children play? Why are nursery rhymes important? Yes, I have met Mexican Americans who knew no nursery rhymes in English or Spanish. These young Chicanos without a childhood who never met their mother's breast gave up their childhood to the fields. Young children who are old enough to walk, hold, and use a hoe were usually in the fields working to earn their way, not because they were told to but because they felt a sense of responsibility to contribute to the family. I have been one of those who knew this world and what is demanded of us and met it head-on.

As time passes, without toys, dolls, and fairy tales, we become adults. The world has received us to compete as adults, we who never had the chance to be children nor the opportunity to be Mexican or American. We are Chicanos because we were forced to take a stand, whatever that may mean to the rest of the world. To us, it means our spirit, pride, and dignity. It is with honor that we wear this badge of Chicano. This pride has led us to positions of leadership with a will to be recognized with a name and individuality.

Am I Mexican, or am I American? How can I be both unless I am split between the two by time? When I was eighteen in 1969, the year of the draft lottery, I was American for the draft. Those honorable and proud Chicanos who died in Vietnam were Americans of Mexican descent. After we were inducted and processed into the military, we became Mexicans, greasers, or spics. You leave home as an American in the morning, and by the time you travel from Portland, Oregon, to Fort Lewis in Tacoma, Washington, that afternoon, your heritage becomes a slur.

We were still willing to serve this country that we believed is a place of opportunity. Why does the pride remain, and the courage fortify that extraordinary will to serve this country that calls you so many names? Names that only those without status and dignity would be called. I guess that at eighteen you put the anger aside and serve while the drill sergeant calls you a grease ball.

As Mexicans, we learned not to oppose authority. My aunts and uncles reminded me not to make waves and to respect those in authority. They might send us back, the older people would say. Organizing, creating unions, and opposing the coyotes who contracted with the farms for our wages and somehow managed to get part of our wages were viewed by my family as communism. The old people told me to stay away from the troublemakers. My Tia Rico said that the farm worker union was filled with communists. After all, only a communist would try to form a labor union.

Mexico, often thought of as the mother of all Mexican Americans (Chicanos), has also turned her back and never welcomed those who left with open arms because of regrets of losing her children. There is so much I could give to the mother soul of all Mexicans, but I will never have the chance to move freely between the two worlds that were imposed onto my spirit. How strange that I belong to a spirit of two worlds, yet I belong to neither. How can I ever find myself and what I am looking for until I figure out where I belong?

I have gone from living in Mexico in a home with clay floors and an outdoor shower with water heated by the sun, making daily trips to the bakery and marketplace, to a home with a pool, a barbecue, a landscaped backyard, and groceries delivered to my home. On this journey, I have crossed several layers of socio-economic strata that often take families numerous generations.

Achieving my professional status was not an easy journey, and there weren't people stumbling over themselves to help me.

While no one achieves success on their own, the network opportunities and access to help are limited for people from lower income brackets. Arriving at my current professional position and economic status, I have constantly faced the struggle to reject assimilation into a mainstream culture that encourages denial and often refuses to recognize the value of non-White racial and ethnic groups. There has been a constant push to absorb the knowledge that would keep me in a helpful position over other human beings. As I sat in my fancy home, I could see, touch, and feel the results of my focused accumulation of things I have been taught to value.

The greatest nation on earth, America, has allowed poverty to flourish; children are now living in starvation. Where are we as a nation? Are we not supposed to oversee our destinies by protecting our future? Poverty now belongs to all races and is no longer the sole possession of African Americans or Mexican Americans, no longer a people-of color-issue. We are in this together and we need to attack this evil condition now. Today, we are faced with racial and ethnic hatred and, in some cases, blatant racism. As we struggle with these challenges, people from our communities have purchased these stereotypes at bargain basement prices.

Our Earth!

Covered, smothered with people crying.

Attics engulfed,

Staring at memories and faded pictures.

Yelling in kitchens, fingers covered in

Dried coffee grounds.

Laughing in basements,

Clothes off, touching each other.

Faces hidden,

Behind lead-covered newspapers,

Waiting, turning to blood.

Hypnotized in TV chairs,

Calloused minds.

Sounds of digital music exploding!

From four-wheeled coffins.

Earth covered with people.

Standing, eyes closed.

On cardboard sidewalks,

Movie theaters, padded leather seats,

Eating, living on herbicidal diets.

Killing insects,

Drowning in liquid from St. Louis,

King of bottled poison.

Scarred arms, swollen veins,

Tracks racing into vomit.

Babies watching,

Virgin eyes learning.

Now the earth was covered with people.

Latinas have always played a critical role in molding me into who I have become. My assimilation into American society accumulated knowledge, observed the use of power, and learned about career mobility, being forced to use credit cards to build credit, and purchasing racial slurs against an already scarce Latino male population. Machismo has become the cocktail word for those mainstream people who have nothing else to worry about. Mainstream people have accumulated enough wealth to allow them to contemplate how family structures in other cultures should function. Wealthy enough to pass judgment on those family structures and decide that all Latino males are machos, whatever that might have meant to them.

Convenience sometimes makes some traits more acceptable than it is at other times. Being macho during World War II and Vietnam was convenient for the comrades-in-arms whose lives were saved by the macho. I am sure it was appreciated by the families of the young men and women who were spared by those heroic acts.

CHAPTER 20
Breaking the Cycle

It is not true that people stop pursuing dreams because they grow old, they grow old because they stop pursuing dreams.

~ Gabriel García Márquez

Not even the wildest of dreams that I had as a child could have predicted where my struggles would take me, what I would accomplish, and the impact I would have on other people. This, however, is not what I meant to accomplish. After this long journey, I have come to realize that true success is not in my status but in the quality of the journey and the need to pass on to others the knowledge gained in a journey of adversity. I am hopeful that these reflections will serve other young people struggling with the unpredictability of the future and of living in a foreign world that does not greet you with arms stretched out, ready to push you away as you get too close.

What all this effort and struggle was about I still do not know or even pretend to understand. It was always my conviction that my voyage was to become someone of prominence, someone who carried a tan year-round, not because I had been working outside all day but because I had been outside playing golf, fly fishing, or out boating on a Sunday afternoon, having the time and money to do it. Becoming someone of prominence would mean that my life had been a success. Yet, knowing when a person becomes somebody (a success) still evades me.

An intellectual way of describing it is on one hand, success could be breaking out of poverty. On the other hand, success has come at a price that has only left me with memories of friends, and dreams of the children I could have raised.

Wisdom may also be a measure of success if a person learns from experience, accepts the knowledge that others are willing to pass on, and is satisfied with the simplicity of silence on this earth with the passion of love in their souls.

Seeking success has propelled me through several social and economic barriers. I have learned how to compete in a mainstream world that has required me to learn behaviors that are not necessarily suited to my culture or my personality but more suited to the nature of competition and living in America. It has been necessary for me to learn how to stay a Mexican in a culturally foreign land known for pressuring citizens to be melted into the pot of the American way of life.

This melting pot theory has caused many young ethnic children confusion in figuring out who they are. The melting pot channels young minds into thinking that they should become someone they can never be. From birth I was raised as a Mexican in every sense of the word from speaking Spanish to Indian healing practices to religion and the strong family relationships with my extended family.

Why is it that when people from different ethnic and cultural backgrounds choose to live in this wonderful country, we call America, we are forced to face the dilemma of denying one culture for another that is often difficult, if not impossible, to define? Isn't it much more valuable for this nation to have citizens expanding their knowledge in more than one language and culture than to spend time and energy trying to get them to forget their native tongues and cultural heritage? What is the logic or the efficiency in learning another language and assimilating another culture to be used as a lever that will only create a lasting internal conflict for having denied who you were since birth?

Like many new arrivals to this land of opportunity, we gradually, over time, begin to question our origins and struggle with who or what we have become. I had to ask myself, where did I come from? I know I have ancestors from Mexico and Spain with most of my heritage stemming from Indigenous people native to what is now called America. It feels disrespectful to describe an entire community as one group when, in reality, there could be people from more than two dozen countries spanning the American continent, the Caribbean, and Spain. We do not all come from the same place and we don't all look alike.

This brings me to Harvard University and the Kennedy School of Government, a university that wasn't even in my thought process as a young boy growing into a young man working the fields of the Pacific Northwest. Harvard was a word and place that never crossed my lips. It was so distant from my daily struggles focused on survival that I had no idea where it was. It was not until I had spent time in the military, got released to go to college, and landed at the University of Oregon (U of O) that I was finally able to look beyond my immediate vision of getting a college degree, so I did not have to continue farm work. The U of O allowed me to open my eyes to curiosity and to question and not to think it was okay just because "We have always done it like this" or as my aunts would remind me, "Don't cause any trouble, mijo."

Education gave me the gift of curiosity, the courage to question, and the determination to find the answers. I went from farmwork to the military, the U of O, to my first professional job, eventually exploring jobs in public service, and eventually drawn to the Alaska pipeline and the utility industry. It was clear that I was not satisfied with many of the things I learned in the private sector and became hungry for more. There was a void in my spirit; I had no purpose. Making money was not enough to fulfill what was driving me to search for more. Whatever that might be, I did not know. While I was working for a major utility and had an income higher than the average worker, I found that my soulful spirit was not being fed. There was a deepening anxiety growing in me to learn more, but I had no idea what I wanted to learn, I just knew that I needed more of what I got at the U of O.

It was time for me to start pursuing what was shadowing me, it was impossible to shake. Being cautious, I began to look at graduate programs in Oregon. I decided to pursue an MBA and apply to Portland State University (PSU), I signed up for the GMAT, filled out the form, and checked the box allowing my score to go out to all the universities; why, I don't know. I remember taking the exam. When I began looking at the MBA program at PSU, unexpectedly I received a letter from Harvard University touting the wonderful program they had at the Kennedy School in Cambridge, Massachusetts.

Hell, I had no idea where Cambridge was and had to look it up on a map. It seemed so far away. I remember putting the letter down and not giving it a second thought. It would be impossible to abandon all the things I had accumulated that gave me a sense of accomplishment. It was much easier to think about driving twenty miles to go to classes and return daily to my custom-built home on five acres with a creek flowing in the back of the property. How could I leave the sight of waking up in the mornings with deer feeding near the back porch or going to the Columbia River only three miles away to fish before going to work?

It was a month later when, out of nowhere, I received a call from a person at Harvard asking me if I had received their letter, and of course, I said yes. The gentleman asked me why they had not heard from me, and I immediately told him I did not have the money to just pack up and go to Massachusetts. There was silence over the phone, and then he broke into loud laughter; I remember thinking, *this man is laughing at me. How disrespectful! He is so rude.* He finally stopped laughing and, in a serious tone, said, "Your problem isn't the money; your problem is getting accepted. If you get accepted, we'll figure out the money."

Suddenly, I remember thinking, *why not?* I decided to apply and began the application and essay. A couple of months later, I received a letter of congratulations in the form of an acceptance letter, and my destiny was forged. Once it became a reality, the lack of money became my reality. I had to sell my pickup. I had never been without a pickup since I could drive. Owning a pickup meant that in the worst of all situations, if I had no job, I always had a pickup that I could use to get jobs hauling things, cutting wood, and selling, or any number of ways to produce an income. I not only sold my pickup but ended up selling my house and everything that had value. The people I worked for seemed to be more excited for me than I was. To me, the unpredictability of where I was going and what this adventure might become eluded me. The people at work, however, were so pleased that they passed the hat to raise money for me. At my going away party, they handed me a grocery bag full of cash. I remember thinking, *how can I leave this place? Everyone is so nice!*

I arrived in Cambridge not knowing a soul, with no place to live and no one to call. My first residence was the YMCA where I fell asleep to night cries of despair, people fighting with each other, and screams for help. After a week of this chaos, I decided to rent a place no matter the cost. As luck would have it, while at the student union with my head down, staring at my morning coffee, I happened to look up and saw two other people with the same blank stare. I wondered if they were in a similar situation. I recall the depressed expression on their faces and could not resist asking them, "Is everything okay?" Simultaneously, they both broke into a chorus, explaining their dilemma of not being able to find housing. My reaction, without thinking, was to suggest that we should look for a place together. I explained that it is easier to find a two- or three-bedroom place than a one bedroom or studio. There was a long pause, and I could see the looks on their faces that said, "Is this guy crazy?" Eventually after finishing a couple cups of coffee and an extended conversation, we all agreed that this could be a good plan. Thus, we began our search for an apartment as potential roommates.

To reduce my costs, I became roommates with an Anglo woman, Lettie, from Nebraska and a Latina, Winnifred or Winnie as we called her, from Colombia. Nettie grew up in Cascade Locks, Oregon, eventually moving to Nebraska and was the daughter of a single mom who was a local judge. Winnie grew up in Bogota, Columbia, until her family moved to Florida. Her mom was a single parent and as the story goes, her father had been a pilot and died in a plane crash.

After a lengthy conversation, we agreed to try and find an apartment together. We knew it would be difficult, but eventually we found a two-bedroom apartment across the river near the Harvard Business School. The three of us were faced with a situation as new friends about which two would get bedrooms and who would get the couch. Our decision was to rotate bedrooms every three months so no one would be on the couch unfairly. It was fate that brought us together and we became inseparable and lifelong friends.

My history of traveling light, coupled with my wanderlust, were the traits that opened the door to a lifelong friendship with two people I would never have met and ended up doing what I thought was a risk. At the time, little did I know that the risk would have been not to take that risk.

Harvard was the best decision I ever made. My experience at Harvard opened my eyes to the larger world around me. I began to realize that the struggles I saw as a boy and the challenges of hunger, poverty, housing, and good-paying jobs were all things that some of the most brilliant people in the world were working on every day. I was exposed to people who were dedicated to fighting for economic equity for people from all walks of life. I learned that I would not be able to solve problems that have always plagued our country by relying on my emotional response. I had to learn to separate my emotions and draw from my intellect in a manner that responded to those emotions positively.

Being at Harvard, I was able to learn from leaders engaged in solving social and economic problems occurring worldwide and sit in classrooms with lecturers who one day would become CEOs of nonprofit organizations, governors, legislators, and secretaries in the executive branch of government, or presidents of foreign countries. But the most important thing I learned was that serving others would be my purpose and mission. Since my time at the Kennedy School, I have dedicated my life to service for those who have historically been ignored and underserved.

I have been able to enter those rooms where the decisions were made on where resources were being allocated to where they would best serve our country, and decisions on what kinds of programs and services would best service our military service members and families, and how to get resources into Indian country. The greatest gift I received from Harvard was the fulfillment of a lifetime struggle to figure out a way to give back to those who guided me to this point.

Exchanging Consciousness

Awareness of each other,

Eternity will never be taken away.

A song in Hell is shrieking,

Echoing, vibrating, tremors of struggle.

Transparency of the minds.

Simulated motions of acceptance,

Explosive rhetoric of change,

A notion of creating an equitable Society.

A futuristic optimism of an institution

At birth, condemned to the acid of Failure.

Creating a new society through CHANGE,

Nature has prohibited.

Without amputating its malignant limb,

The infection will spread further.

The tune of the song is different,

The words are the same.

To change the song, you need to change.

The tune and the words.

Lonely bird flies like a white pearl,

Floating.

In a blue turquoise sea

A flight with no destination.

Freedom from being alone.

Endless flight ends as it begins,

Loneliness becomes its shadow.

Magnifying every movement, being watched,

Scientist conducting experiments.

Little bird, stay where you are.

Endless cycle of life, chasing the sun,
Eternity circling the earth.
Foolish fowl scorched by life,
Blown to dust, chasing the universe.
Returning to the nest where it was given life.
Your journey will end where you begin,
Caught!
In society's straight jacket,
Arms, overlap, muscles tense,
Exhausted, trying to escape.
Subtle hints. Asking me to give up,
What is unknown to me, demanding,
That I do not search, the unknown reality.
Pushing, pulling, yanking,
At every breath taken by undetectable lungs.
Smothered! Close to suffocation.
Rebellion is left.
A swift snake uncoils, strikes,
Attempts of resort are taken.
Attacking, the enemy in patent leather shoes,

Scuffing the shine of bloodied shoes,

Revealing a face

Reflections of a mirror.

Fear, biting at our heels,

Knowing they had given of themselves.

A spirit sealed to cement monasteries,

Attempting to take mine away!

CHAPTER 21
Madre and a Full Circle

There's a unique sadness in missing someone who should always be there, but for some reason, isn't.
~ Unknown

You might have noticed the distinct lack of my mother's presence in these chapters. Here, she resurrects. Yes, I do have a mother, and I found her later-in-life after searching for about a year.

While I was always surrounded by aunts, uncles, cousins, and many extended family members in my childhood, I began to wonder about my mother as I grew older. My earliest memories are of sweet milk seeping through my clinched lips, small and tight, not wanting to let go of the nipple of nourishment that I was taking in. Recollections of my mother were only of warm milk touching my face as it overflowed from my mouth when I suckled too much.

And then, a void appeared where my mother should have been. Despite the outpouring of loving kindness from other female surrogates in my formative years, I realize now that I've always had this desperate hunger and have never known when I've had enough. I wonder how many motherless sons mourn upon reading the Moroccan proverb: "Every beetle is a gazelle in the eyes of its mother." There is no true substitute for the unconditional, primal support a mother gives. When it's absent, no matter the best efforts of relatives, a wound is left. It might heal, but the scar never fades.

She had never been around, and I heard not a word about her or her absence from our family. It was as if there was never a mother. Instead, as I've mentioned, I had my dad's older sisters who, by default, cared for me and my siblings as immediate relatives from the time my grandparents died and left my dad's siblings orphaned. My aunts were always there to watch over and protect us and make sure we had whatever we needed.

It was as if my mother had never been a part of our lives. I always had more than enough love and support, and it was unimaginable to miss someone I had never known or even known existed. I was lucky to have the power and strength of my extended family. Who knows what would have happened to me and my brother and sisters without their support.

Very infrequently—and I mean so infrequently that I can barely remember—she would flit in and out of our lives. She had her reasons, which were never adequately explained to my siblings and me. The last time I saw my mother, she was arguing with my father as he pointed a pistol in her direction. It was Christmas Day, with small gifts sitting on the bed waiting to be unwrapped.

"Dad," I cried out. "Please stop." I walked toward him, then crawled on top of a hundred-pound bag of pinto beans on the kitchen floor, reaching over to grab the tip of the pistol barrel. "Please don't do that."

In amazement, my father began to cry and lowered the pistol, yelling obscenities as he walked out of the little shack we lived in. The yelling didn't stop even when he reached the car. What's so remarkable is that I understood why this happened. I had seen my mother with another man in bed just before my father entered the house. It is no wonder that I would be confused about love and relationships.

***

It was soon after my fortieth birthday and after more than six years of working in Washington D.C. that I decided to return to my hometown in Eagle Pass, Texas, to revisit where part of my journey began. While in Eagle Pass, I developed this burning notion that it was time to find my mother and finally get to know her. The challenge was that I had no clue where she was, where she had lived, or anything about her past. I had no idea of her background because while growing up no one ever mentioned anything good or bad about my mother. So, when I started to look for her, I had no idea where to begin.

Eagle Pass and Piedras Negras seemed the easiest starting point. This was where my aunts and uncles lived, and where it all began. They had spent a lifetime raising me and would surely know something. But when I began asking questions, it was clear that my family had not kept a connection with my mother or her whereabouts. All they could offer were distant memories of her relatives and where they used to live. So, the journey began with me making a list of relatives on my mother's side and visiting the communities where they had lived.

I found myself driving to small towns in northern Mexico, knocking on doors and asking about my relatives, only to find they no longer lived there and had moved decades prior. I drove from northern Mexico into communities along the U.S.-Mexico border from small town to another until one day, I knocked on a door, and a lovely woman answered with kind eyes staring at me as if she knew me. I went ahead to tell her the story about my mother and my efforts to try and track her down.

She listened patiently until I was finished and said, "Yes, I knew your mother, but I don't know where she is today." And she went ahead to tell me that my mother had a twin sister who lived in Chicago and that there was a Vasquez family that lived in Uvalde that might be connected to our family.

I decided to try to find my mother's twin sister in Chicago, and at that time, there were still information operators in the phone system who could look up names and give you their phone numbers. As luck would have it, I reached out to an operator to request a listing, and she told me there was a number with that name, but she could not give me the number because it was an unlisted number, which meant the information could not be released.

Not knowing what to do and in desperation, I begged the operator to listen to my story and decide whether she could give me the number or call that number and convey the story to my aunt to see if she would be willing to call me. In the back of my mind, I was thinking, *this lady is not going to call my aunt and take the time to tell her the whole story, and I won't be able to find my mother this way.* All the while, I was planning my next move and considering the next community to visit.

Imagine my surprise when my aunt called me, and I quickly realized that the operator, through the kindness of her heart, shared the entire story, prompting my aunt Julia to promptly call me. From our first conversation, I planned a trip to Chicago to visit her the following month. When I arrived, I was greeted by my cousin Vira who did not hesitate to tell me they had planned a small gathering so I could meet my other uncles and cousins on my mother's side, whom I had never met before. When we finally all came together, it was uncanny how I looked so much like my uncles, which is something that brought some closure because I really did not bear any resemblance to my uncles on my father's side.

The visit with my mother's family brought me a certain level of peace and balance that I hadn't known was missing. The visit also pointed me to the direction of where my mother was living, and to my surprise, it was just across the border from Eagle Pass and only a quarter mile from the checkpoint into Mexico. I decided to make the trip to Piedras Negras and surprise my mother with the visit, which may not have been the best of ideas. But it was all I could think about at the time.

So, I made the trip back to Eagle Pass across the border into Piedras Negras to the street where my mother lived. I walked up to the door full of anxiety, knocking several times until a young woman greeted me. I later found out this was my sister. She was my sister because children born from the same mother are considered full siblings. I later found out that I had five other brothers and sisters whom I had not met.

My sister Lourdes took me into the kitchen where my mother was sitting, and I introduced myself as her son. The first thing she asked me was, "What do you want?" My response was that I did not want anything and that I was there because she needed to meet us, meaning myself and my other brothers and sisters in the United States.

Our first meeting together was filled with caution, like crossing a field of landmines and having to be careful of every word and phrase in order not to offend. From that first meeting, I went back and forth several times throughout the week just to gradually get to know her until it was time to return to Virginia. Once back in the D.C., area, I made it a point to go back and visit my mother on a regular basis.

After a couple of years of getting to know each other, during one particular visit my mother became teary-eyed and confessed that most of her life, she had been a terribly angry and bitter woman. But since my first visit, followed by my siblings, she began to feel peace and enjoy life for the first time. She became more affectionate and added to our discussions, and it also gave me a profound sense of peace and comfort.

I consider it a full-circle event, from birth to three-quarters of a century of life, now fuller because I found my mother.

CONCLUSION

Latinos have lived in what is now the United States since the sixteenth century. In the early 1800s, when the United States annexed Florida, Louisiana, and the northern half of Mexico, more than 100,000 Spanish-speaking residents became U.S. citizens. The 1850 U.S. census, taken shortly after the conquest of Mexico, counted more than 80,000 former Mexicans, 2,000 Cubans and Puerto Ricans, and another 20,000 people from Central and South America. Today, the descendants of those 1850 citizens are part of a Latino population that has grown enormously. As of 2017, more than 58 million Americans claimed Latin American heritage. See Latinx Great Migrations - History and Geography at depts.washington.edu/labhist for an in-depth dive into the past.

As reported by the PEW Research center, the U.S. Hispanic population reached 63.6 million in 2022, up from 50.5 million in 2010. The 26% increase in the Hispanic population was faster than the nation's 8% growth rate but slower than the 34% increase in the Asian population. In 2022, Hispanics made up nearly one-in-five people in the U.S. (19%), up from 16% in 2010 and just 5% in 1970.

The intricacy of a human being's makeup emerges and evolves over time. My very existence has been a disconnected dance between the decisions that molded me and the elusive essence of the rapidly changing environment in the U.S. and the world. As I reflect on the metamorphosis of my identity, I'm haunted by persistent questions that elude many young immigrants: who am I and when did this transformation occur? Is it a compilation of influences from myriad souls, experiences, and knowledge traversing my life, or is it an ancestral echo, a whisper of secrets handed down through the tapestry of generations?

Throughout my journey and finally, in my later years, the questions that haunted me at an early age have transformed beyond the original inquiry to reveal some logic toward self-realization. Yet, I'm bewildered with new questions in the wake of the accumulation of knowledge. How can the ledger of my life remain with a balance of more questions than answers? My unresolved internal queries reveal themselves from within as turmoil, anger, and an unyielding urge to conquer the uncharted challenge of finding resolution.

The genesis of my unanswered questions remains elusive, a nebulous origin that eludes definition. I've discerned only that many young Mexican Americans share this labyrinth, navigating a path where the label "Mexican" may brand them as outcasts and claiming "American" may cast them as traitors, and identifying as indigenous is quickly dismissed. Why, after centuries of existence in the U.S., are we viewed as new arrivals (immigrants) to land we inhabited as Indigenous people before the Spaniards and as Latinos since the early 1600s? As an Indigenous people, we were present on this land long before the establishment of the U.S.

Given the Latino presence in every state in the country, I wonder why young Latinos must ask themselves, *what is my name? José or Joe? Why do my parents and family call me José, while teachers and peers favor Joe? Why was it important to change our names to go to grade school? How difficult is it to pronounce Juan instead of John? When did this name change us, and in that transition, what fragments of our identity were sacrificed?*

In my youth, I began to feel a growing anxiety adjusting to our life and a new culture while having no understanding as to why our language, beginning with our names, could not be used as part of our transition to life in America. As I grew older, learned more, and obtained greater education, I realized that adjusting our perception of ourselves and the use of our language became a critical piece of the "Melting Pot" notion of becoming an American. I started to understand why I got a whack on the back of the hand when I spoke Spanish to the only Mexican kid in my class. This was the beginning of a process of colonization which begins by controlling the language of someone "different," meaning someone from another country and another culture.

As I mentioned, in the years of my transition I've been called spic, greaser, wetback, Hispanic, Latinx, and Latine. It was never clear what group of people engaged in the attempts to change or manipulate our identities. This was a question that I deliberately sought to understand and, as of today, have still not been able to figure out other than what has happened in other parts of the world where nations sought to conquer and control entire cultures and civilizations.

While I am only an amateur researcher, I have been an astute observer of life and am a student of history. Thus, I have realized that eliminating a culture's language is in the critical path of colonization. I recently came across an article by Ananya Ravishankar titled "Linguistic Imperialism: Colonial Violence through Language," The Trinity Papers (2011 - present) (2020). Its introduction was succinct and touched on some of my intuitive thoughts that I have had over the years, as follows:

> *Language is by no means an arbitrary fact of the world, similarly, it is also not any arbitrary fact of colonialism. We ought to consider it as another form of violence imposed upon cultures by colonial rule, as devastatingly treacherous as any other. Of course, there is an obvious distinction between physical and linguistic subjugation, and the previous claim is not to erase this in any element. Linguistic violence itself persists long past the departure of the colonist, it is a violence committed against a very culture, one from which it may never fully recover. Language is not merely a group of symbols or words; this is clear from the fact that we see it as having been the object*

> *of colonial assault. Imperial powers recognized it as anything but arbitrary, else it would not have even been seen as necessary to be subject to the same ravage. We ought not to let the role of language in colonialism slip into the background for the sake of a seemingly more urgent or significant aspect of it. Language as a means of colonial dominance has too often been seen as "one of many symptoms of a larger colonial pathology" (Flores, Rodriguez 2012, 27), as a side-effect that does not require to be dealt with urgently or with equal dedication as with more wide-spread and common conceptions of colonial violence.*

The survival of my identity was to hold close to my spirit and soul the lessons and words shared with me by my elders. At an early age, my family reinforced the importance of my language, ancestry, culture, and origin. It has been the matriarchs of my family who reminded me daily that I descended from a people that created one of the largest civilizations of its time and possessed architects, scientists, mathematicians, artists, poets, farmers, and craftspeople with many more aspects of the culture reflected in the America of today. We see it in buildings, food, art, and throughout the general population. My matriarchs reinforced that as a people we would not fade into the way of assimilation but that our assimilation would transition us into the civilization that had been prophesied.

My aunts, but mostly my uncles, provided me with the lessons of survival in an environment they knew would not be so welcoming. They grew up in a time that rejected the notion of people who were of color and not European, White, or Protestant. Their youth taught them to always walk with caution anytime they left the boundaries of the colonia (the community neighborhood where families and friends congregated, creating a community within a community). In their youth, it was openly announced that they were not welcome. It was common to see signs above water fountains that indicated "For Whites Only" or "No Mexicans or Dogs Allowed."

It is no wonder that my uncles wanted me to learn to defend myself. They taught me how to overcome my fear and never back down from a fight. Over time, I learned the true lesson: it was not the ability to fight physically but the spirit of not being swayed by threats and fighting for what I believed was worth fighting for. Although I did learn how to defend myself physically, those lessons also provided an ability to defend myself through words and strategy.

Evening campfires in my early migrant years planted seeds that would eventually define my identity, the lessons blossoming within the stories. These recollections guided me during my times of confusion about self-worth. The old people helped ground me in the understanding that I would be traveling into a world that would provide new knowledge and understanding of the larger world. From an early age, I was aware that I would venture into a world that would not be so welcoming but would offer a diversity of people. It would also offer knowledge that would be part of creating a more advanced and peaceful world.

Like in the ancient Indian prophecy, my family would become part of the assimilation that would welcome the merging of families from other nations, cultures, and races. As a family, we were scattered throughout Mexico and the Western parts of the states. Since the time of the conquest and the abandonment of the ancient cities, we have seen our people migrate back and forth to the ancient lands, with many settling in some of the ancient lands as far north as California, Oregon, and Washington to Illinois, Missouri, and Florida. From the time of the abandonment of the ancient cities to today, you can observe the visual impact of what had been foreseen.

My transition through life has provided me with an abundance of knowledge gained through trial and error, coupled with practical experience from working at many different jobs and occupations from the time I could hold a hoe. Going to school in the U.S. added another layer of knowledge, fluency in another language, and the ability to conceptualize from a different lens. It challenged my mind to consciously translate one language into another while ensuring the communications' conceptual framework was aligned with the intent.

At first, it was difficult, if not stressful, to consciously think about what was being said, which meant that it made sense. And, of course, there was the dilemma of shedding this accent that came from centuries of Indian dialogue mixed with a bit of Spanish. I guess if you stop to think about it, I might have appeared to be quite a mess to my teachers. After three years of intensive phonetics and speech therapy in a learning-disabled class, my accent miraculously disappeared. From that point on I had little to no difficulty reading. However, it took a bit longer to realize that the written words and concepts did not always translate as intended. After a few more years of practice and further education at the university level, I expanded my ability to think more critically.

My experience at the University of Oregon opened the doors to exploring the many radical thoughts that had been haunting me from childhood. Questions like why some people in the richest country had to live in places and under conditions that resembled some of the poorest places I had seen in Mexico. I began to understand how politics critically impacted every aspect of life and was impossible to ignore. I quickly went from a young man happy to have the opportunity to be at the university to an angry radical who began to question every aspect of government involvement.

It seems as if there was nothing that the government had not touched. The only course of action for a young Latino or Chicano, as we referred to ourselves at the time, was to get involved in movements that supported the worker, and for me, the cause was that of the farmworker. It seems that the more I learned the angrier I got. There appeared to be no recourse other than revolution. Yes, and as you may have already figured out, a bunch of college kids could not succeed in making a radical change, but we learned that we could influence and sometimes shift the impact of government involvement.

The University of Oregon brought out the best in my creative thinking, providing me with the tools to think critically and not accept what was on the surface but rather turn over a few stones to assess what was happening underneath. Beyond the expansion of my mind, the U of O taught me how to organize and mobilize efforts with diverse groups. I got involved with African American, Asian, Native American, Middle Eastern, and Latino students with similar passions. At the time, we did not believe in what our government was doing but did believe in what our country stood for—freedom and opportunity. I was one of the few students who had already served in the military, and I always felt as if I had earned the right to protest. God Bless America! I am still protesting. At the undergraduate level, I received the tools that prepared me to take on the socio-economic challenges facing the poor. What it did not prepare me for was how to get it done.

As for graduate school, I don't know how it happened, and I will never know, but I ended up at Harvard Kennedy School (HKS) of Government. On reflection, it was a blessing in that it put me on track to positive change and off the path to self-destruction because of my impatience and need to see and feel social and economic justice. Now! While at HKS, I met people from all over the world who had lived through similar challenges, if not worse, and they seemed to have developed a more guided approach with uncommon patience. I remember thinking, *how can people have such a clear vision of where they need to go and remain so hopeful, without anger and bitterness?* They are better people than me. I wanted to be like those leaders who understood what they needed to do and how to get it done. I believe I learned the fine art of "getting it done" through the combination of early campfires, life experience, military service, education, and last but not least, the curandera that foretold I would end up doing something important and impactful.

I was blessed to serve two terms with the Clinton administration and the Obama administration and work my way up from writing briefing books for the White House to Deputy Assistant Secretary of Defense for the Office of the Secretary and Deputy Under Secretary in Rural Development for the Department of Agriculture. The time I spent in Washington D.C. allowed me to serve the Native American population across the country, the people of the Mississippi Delta (mostly the African American community), the Appalachia region that provided for our energy needs for decades and was later abandoned, and the Southwest border region—my place of origin and where over two-thirds of the Latinos in the U.S. reside.

My work in Washington D.C. showed me that many people in this country have experienced a similar journey to mine and that the only way that I am special is that I live in America and eventually ended up in a place to give back as I was taught. The biggest lesson I learned is that this great country is made up of many different immigrants, and they all had the same struggles when they first arrived. What is different for those of Aztec descent is that we are called immigrants, but we did not migrate here. We were already here and were given citizenship when the United States signed the Treaty of Guadalupe Hidalgo. That treaty gave many guarantees that we have insisted on keeping such as our language.

After hundreds of years of living, exploring, and advancing the development of what is now the U.S., people still look into our eyes and consider us immigrants. It wasn't that long ago when a presidential candidate, on the first day of launching his campaign, said, "They are not our friend, believe me," before disparaging Mexican immigrants: "They're bringing drugs. They're bringing crime. They're rapists. And some, I assume, are good people." Several networks such as ABC, CBS, CNN, and most major newspapers reported this in the news. It was just the beginning of the attacks on people from Mexico that later expanded to most immigrants of color. Most recently, the same candidate who is running for the presidency once more accused the immigrants of poisoning their blood. Whoever they are, I believe that their blood has already been poisoned with hate and violence.

I recall a conversation I had with my thirteen-year-old daughter who was watching when the presidential election results of 2016 came across the screen. She remained with me until we had the results. To my dismay, the people of America elected an individual to the presidency with no public service or military experience. When the votes were finally all counted, and we knew that it was finally over, my daughter looked at me and asked, "What does that mean for me?" This was the most difficult question that anyone had ever asked me. I had no answer for her, and I felt like I had let her down because I knew that I could not protect her from someone who had such disregard for women that he could laugh and joke about grabbing them in a vulgar and disgusting manner.

I had never felt helpless when it came to protecting my family, and as I contemplated the question from my daughter, all I could do was cry. It was difficult to understand why a proven leader—a woman—could not get elected. Why is there so much resistance to having a woman lead our country? It was the first time that I began to consider, as a person of another culture and a man of color, that it was more difficult to achieve equity as a woman. God help the women of color!

In 2024, I found myself living in an environment that is more threatening to Latinos and people of color than it was in the 1960s when I was a teenager. How, after centuries of inhabiting this continent, are we viewed as immigrants just because of our language and color? Having traveled to every state in the country and personally driven through countless towns, cities, and counties with Spanish origin names that number in the hundreds. We tend to forget that seven of our states—Arizona, California, Colorado, Florida, Nevada, New Mexico, and Texas—came from a mix of Spanish and Mexica origin.

A 2022 report by the Joint Economic Committee states the total economic output of the Latino population of the U. S. was estimated to be $2 trillion. This included five million businesses that contribute $800 billion every year to the national economy. The number of Latino-owned businesses between 2012 and 2017 in the U.S. grew by 14%, which was more than twice the national average. According to McKinsey & Company, they also account for the fastest-growing portion of the U. S. GDP. So much so that if the American Latinos had their own country, they would have the highest GDP growth in the past decade after China and India.

As a people, we are now deeply integrated into this country. In a Pew Report (February 11, 2008, U.S. Population Projections: 2005-2050 by Jeffery S. Passel and D'Vera Cohn), they project that by 2050, the nation's racial and ethnic mix will look quite different than it does now. Non-Hispanic Whites, who made up 67% of the population in 2005, will be 47% in 2050. Hispanics will rise from 14% of the population in 2005 to 29% in 2050. Black people at 13% of the population in 2005 will be roughly the same proportion in 2050. Asians, who were 5% of the population in 2005, will be 9% in 2050.

Today, as I do the final review and edit of this autofiction, I can write that, for the moment, I am hopeful that Americans from all walks of life have come to the realization that we cannot go the way of lies, anger, and hatred. We must listen to our young Americans who have lived in a world that has already accepted the notion that diversity in language, race, and culture benefits America and the world. We are all one as human being, and we are participants in the evolution of humanity.

This brings us full circle to the stories I learned over a campfire about how we would eventually regain our ancient lands and become a people of multiple races.

ABOUT THE AUTHOR

Victor Vasquez was born in Mexico in 1949 into a family of migrant workers. As a child, he learned the ancient lore of his people while gathering around campfires and harvesting crops in the U.S. He juxtaposed these experiences against life in Oregon, where his father settled the family and enrolled Victor in a predominantly White elementary school.

Integrating into English-only academics was a struggle, and integrating into an unfamiliar culture was even more challenging. Poverty, prejudice, an absent mother, an overworked father, and dependent siblings had Victor working odd jobs from an early age to help support the family. A stint in junior high and high school sports helped counterbalance a rebellious streak as he made his way toward graduation, only to be told by a school counselor that he wasn't "college material."

Victor proved the school counselor wrong by enrolling in Blue Mountain Community College, enlisting, and serving honorably in the Army as his father and uncles had, and graduating from the University of Oregon. He earned a master's degree at Harvard University's Kennedy School of Government and, over the span of thirty years, became a public servant. He served two terms with the Clinton and Obama administrations and worked his way up from writing briefing books for the White House to Deputy Assistant Secretary of Defense for the Office of the Secretary and Deputy Under Secretary in Rural Development for the Department of Agriculture. His focus was on Native American populations across the country, the people of the Mississippi Delta (mostly the African American Community), the Appalachia region that provided for our energy needs for decades and was later abandoned, and the

Southwest border region—his place of origin and where over two-thirds of the Latinos in the U.S. reside.

Today, Victor studies the roots of his lineage and prophecies stretching back to Aztec rule. Within his memoir, *A Fly in Milk (Una Mosca En La Leche)*, he shares original poetry and ponders the state of humanity, wondering when his ancient people will finally be called home.

www.ingramcontent.com/pod-product-compliance
Lightning Source LLC
LaVergne TN
LVHW010645110826
845149LV00014B/2962

* 9 7 8 1 9 5 9 4 4 6 3 8 5 *